# Four Corners

## Jack C. Richards · David Bohlke

# 2B

## Student's Book

CAMBRIDGE
UNIVERSITY PRESS

# CAMBRIDGE
## UNIVERSITY PRESS

32 Avenue of the Americas, New York, NY 10013-2473, USA

Cambridge University Press is part of the University of Cambridge.

It furthers the University's mission by disseminating knowledge in the pursuit of education, learning and research at the highest international levels of excellence.

www.cambridge.org
Information on this title: www.cambridge.org/9780521126717

© Cambridge University Press 2011

First published 2011
4th printing 2016

Printed in Italy by Rotolito Lombarda S.p.A.

*A catalogue record for this publication is available from the British Library*

ISBN  978-0-521-12668-7  Full Contact 2A with Self-study CD-ROM
ISBN  978-0-521-12671-7  Full Contact 2B with Self-study CD-ROM
ISBN  978-0-521-12688-5  Teacher's Edition 2 with Assessment Audio CD / CD-ROM
ISBN  978-0-521-12681-6  Class Audio CDs 2
ISBN  978-0-521-12663-2  Classware 2
ISBN  978-0-521-12677-9  DVD 2

For a full list of components, visit www.cambridge.org/fourcorners

Cambridge University Press has no responsibility for the persistence or accuracy of URLs for external or third-party internet websites referred to in this publication, and does not guarantee that any content on such websites is, or will remain, accurate or appropriate. Information regarding prices, travel timetables, and other factual information given in this work is correct at the time of first printing but Cambridge University Press does not guarantee the accuracy of such information thereafter.

Art direction, book design, photo research, and layout services: Adventure House, NYC
Audio production: CityVox, NYC
Video production: Steadman Productions

# Authors' acknowledgments

Many people contributed to the development of *Four Corners*. The authors and publisher would like to particularly thank the following **reviewers**:

Nele Noe, **Academy for Educational Development, Qatar Independent Secondary School for Girls**, Doha, Qatar; Yuan-hsun Chuang, **Soo Chow University**, Taipei, Taiwan; Celso Frade and Sonia Maria Baccari de Godoy, **Associaçao Alumni**, São Paulo, Brazil; Pablo Stucchi, **Antonio Raimondi School** and **Instituto San Ignacio de Loyola**, Lima, Peru; Kari Miller, **Binational Center**, Quito, Ecuador; Alex K. Oliveira, **Boston University**, Boston, MA, USA; Elisabeth Blom, **Casa Thomas Jefferson**, Brasilia, Brazil; Henry Grant, **CCBEU – Campinas**, Campinas, Brazil; Maria do Rosário, **CCBEU – Franca**, Franca, Brazil; Ane Cibele Palma, **CCBEU Inter Americano**, Curitiba, Brazil; Elen Flavia Penques da Costa, **Centro de Cultura Idiomas – Taubate**, Taubate, Brazil; Inara Lúcia Castillo Couto, **CEL LEP – São Paulo**, São Paulo, Brazil; Geysa de Azevedo Moreira, **Centro Cultural Brasil Estados Unidos (CCBEU Belém)**, Belém, Brazil; Sonia Patricia Cardoso, **Centro de Idiomas Universidad Manuela Beltrán**, Barrio Cedritos, Colombia; Geraldine Itiago Losada, **Centro Universitario Grupo Sol (Musali)**, Mexico City, Mexico; Nick Hilmers, **DePaul University**, Chicago, IL, USA; Monica L. Montemayor Menchaca, **EDIMSA**, Metepec, Mexico; Angela Whitby, **Edu-Idiomas Language School**, Cholula, Puebla, Mexico; Mary Segovia, **El Monte Rosemead Adult School**, Rosemead, CA, USA; Dr. Deborah Aldred, **ELS Language Centers, Middle East Region**, Abu Dhabi, United Arab Emirates; Leslie Lott, **Embassy CES**, Ft. Lauderdale, FL, USA; M. Martha Lengeling, **Escuela de Idiomas**, Guanajuato, Mexico; Pablo Frias, **Escuela de Idiomas UNAPEC**, Santo Domingo, Dominican Republic; Tracy Vanderhoek, **ESL Language Center**, Toronto, Canada; Kris Vicca and Michael McCollister, **Feng Chia University**, Taichung, Taiwan; Flávia Patricia do Nascimento Martins, **First Idiomas**, Sorocaba, Brazil; Andrea Taylor, **Florida State University in Panama**, Panamá, Panama; Carlos Lizárraga González, **Groupo Educativo Angloamericano**, Mexico City, Mexico; Dr. Martin Endley, **Hanyang University**, Seoul, Korea; Mauro Luiz Pinheiro, **IBEU Ceará**, Ceará, Brazil; Ana Lúcia da Costa Maia de Almeida, **IBEU Copacabana**, Copacabana, Brazil; Ana Lucia Almeida, Elisa Borges, **IBEU Rio**, Rio de Janeiro, Brazil; Maristela Silva, **ICBEU Manaus**, Manaus, Brazil; Magaly Mendes Lemos, **ICBEU São José dos Campos**, São José dos Campos, Brazil; Augusto Pelligrini Filho, **ICBEU São Luis**, São Luis, Brazil; Leonardo Mercado, **ICPNA**, Lima, Peru; Lucia Rangel Lugo, **Instituto Tecnológico de San Luis Potosí**, San Luis Potosí, Mexico; Maria Guadalupe Hernández Lozada, **Instituto Tecnológico de Tlalnepantla**, Tlalnepantla de Baz, Mexico; Greg Jankunis, **International Education Service**, Tokyo, Japan; Karen Stewart, **International House Veracruz**, Veracruz, Mexico; George Truscott, **Kinki University**, Osaka, Japan; Bo-Kyung Lee, **Hankuk University of Foreign Studies**, Seoul, Korea; Andy Burki, **Korea University, International Foreign Language School**, Seoul, Korea; Jinseo Noh, **Kwangwoon University**, Seoul, Korea; Nadezhda Nazarenko, **Lone Star College**, Houston, TX, USA; Carolyn Ho, **Lone Star College-Cy-Fair**, Cypress, TX, USA; Alice Ya-fen Chou, **National Taiwan University of Science and Technology**, Taipei, Taiwan; Gregory Hadley, **Niigata University of International and Information Studies, Department of Information Culture**, Niigata-shi, Japan; Raymond Dreyer, **Northern Essex Community College**, Lawrence, MA, USA; Mary Keter Terzian Megale, **One Way Línguas-Suzano**, São Paulo, Brazil; Jason Moser, **Osaka Shoin Joshi University**, Kashiba-shi, Japan; Bonnie Cheeseman, **Pasadena Community College** and **UCLA American Language Center**, Los Angeles, CA, USA; Simon Banha, **Phil Young's English School**, Curitiba, Brazil; Oh Jun Il, **Pukyong National University**, Busan, Korea; Carmen Gehrke, **Quatrum English Schools**, Porto Alegre, Brazil; Atsuko K. Yamazaki, **Shibaura Institute of Technology**, Saitama, Japan; Wen hsiang Su, **Shi Chien University, Kaohsiung Campus**, Kaohsiung, Taiwan; Richmond Stroupe, **Soka University, World Language Center**, Hachioji, Tokyo, Japan; Lynne Kim, **Sun Moon University (Institute for Language Education)**, Cheon An City, Chung Nam, Korea; Hiroko Nishikage, **Taisho University**, Tokyo, Japan; Diaña Peña Munoz and Zaira Kuri, **The Anglo**, Mexico City, Mexico; Alistair Campbell, **Tokyo University of Technology**, Tokyo, Japan; Song-won Kim, **TTI (Teacher's Training Institute)**, Seoul, Korea; Nancy Alarcón, **UNAM FES Zaragoza Language Center**, Mexico City, Mexico; Laura Emilia Fierro López, **Universidad Autónoma de Baja California**, Mexicali, Mexico; María del Rocío Domíngeuz Gaona, **Universidad Autónoma de Baja California**, Tijuana, Mexico; Saul Santos Garcia, **Universidad Autónoma de Nayarit**, Nayarit, Mexico; Christian Meléndez, **Universidad Católica de El Salvador**, San Salvador, El Salvador; Irasema Mora Pablo, **Universidad de Guanajuato**, Guanajuato, Mexico; Alberto Peto, **Universidad de Oxaca**, Tehuantepec, Mexico; Carolina Rodriguez Beltan, **Universidad Manuela Beltrán, Centro Colombo Americano**, and **Universidad Jorge Tadeo Lozano**, Bogotá, Colombia; Nidia Milena Molina Rodriguez, **Universidad Manuela Beltrán** and **Universidad Militar Nueva Granada**, Bogotá, Colombia; Yolima Perez Arias, **Universidad Nacional de Colombia**, Bogota, Colombia; Héctor Vázquez García, **Universidad Nacional Autónoma de Mexico**, Mexico City, Mexico; Pilar Barrera, **Universidad Técnica de Ambato**, Ambato, Ecuador; Deborah Hulston, **University of Regina**, Regina, Canada; Rebecca J. Shelton, **Valparaiso University, Interlink Language Center**, Valparaiso, IN, USA; Tae Lee, **Yonsei University**, Seodaemun-gu, Seoul, Korea; Claudia Thereza Nascimento Mendes, **York Language Institute**, Rio de Janeiro, Brazil; Jamila Jenny Hakam, **ELT Consultant**, Muscat, Oman; Stephanie Smith, **ELT Consultant**, Austin, TX, USA.

The authors would also like to thank the Four Corners editorial, production, and new media teams, as well as the Cambridge University Press staff and advisors around the world for their contributions and tireless commitment to quality.

# Scope and sequence

| LEVEL 2B | Learning outcomes | Grammar | Vocabulary |
|---|---|---|---|
| **Unit 7**     Pages 65–74 | | | |
| **Shopping**<br>A *It's lighter and thinner.*<br>B *Would you take $10?*<br>C *This hat is too small.*<br>D *A shopper's paradise* | **Students can . . .**<br>☑ describe and compare products<br>☑ bargain<br>☑ describe how clothing looks and fits<br>☑ discuss good places to shop | Comparative adjectives<br>*Enough* and *too* | Opposites<br>Adjectives to describe<br>  clothing |
| **Unit 8**     Pages 75–84 | | | |
| **Fun in the city**<br>A *You shouldn't miss it!*<br>B *I'd recommend going . . .*<br>C *The best and the worst*<br>D *The best place to go* | **Students can . . .**<br>☑ say what people should do in a city<br>☑ ask for and give a recommendation<br>☑ make comparisons about their city<br>☑ discuss aspects of a city | *Should* for<br>  recommendations; *can*<br>  for possibility<br>Superlative adjectives | Places to see<br>Adjectives to describe<br>  cities |
| **Unit 9**     Pages 85–94 | | | |
| **People**<br>A *Where was he born?*<br>B *I'm not sure, but I think . . .*<br>C *People I admire*<br>D *Making a difference* | **Students can . . .**<br>☑ ask and talk about people from the past<br>☑ express certainty and uncertainty<br>☑ describe people they admire<br>☑ describe people who made a difference | *Was / Were born*; past<br>  of *be*<br>Simple past; *ago* | Careers<br>Personality adjectives |
| **Unit 10**     Pages 95–104 | | | |
| **In a restaurant**<br>A *The ice cream is fantastic!*<br>B *I'll have the fish, please.*<br>C *Have you ever . . . ?*<br>D *Restaurant experiences* | **Students can . . .**<br>☑ talk about menus and eating out<br>☑ order food in a restaurant<br>☑ ask about and describe food experiences<br>☑ describe restaurant experiences | Articles<br>Present perfect for<br>  experience | Menu items<br>Interesting food |
| **Unit 11**     Pages 105–114 | | | |
| **Entertainment**<br>A *I'm not a fan of dramas.*<br>B *Any suggestions?*<br>C *All of us love music.*<br>D *Musicians from around the world* | **Students can . . .**<br>☑ talk about their movie habits and opinions<br>☑ ask for and give suggestions<br>☑ report the results of a survey<br>☑ describe important singers and musicians | *So, too, either*, and *neither*<br>Determiners | Types of movies<br>Types of music |
| **Unit 12**     Pages 115–124 | | | |
| **Time for a change**<br>A *Personal change*<br>B *I'm happy to hear that!*<br>C *I think I'll get a job.*<br>D *Dreams and aspirations* | **Students can . . .**<br>☑ give reasons for personal changes<br>☑ react to good and bad news<br>☑ make predictions about the future<br>☑ discuss their dreams for the future | Infinitives of purpose<br>*Will* for predictions; *may,*<br>  *might* for possibility | Personal goals<br>Milestones |

| Functional language | Listening and Pronunciation | Reading and Writing | Speaking |
|---|---|---|---|
| **Interactions:**<br>Bargaining for a lower price<br>Suggesting a different price | **Listening:**<br>Bargaining at a yard sale<br>A weekend market in London<br>**Pronunciation:**<br>Linked sounds | **Reading:**<br>"Chatuchak Weekend Market"<br>A webpage<br>**Writing:**<br>An interesting market | • Comparison of products<br>• *Keep talking:* Three products<br>• Role play of a bargaining situation<br>• Discussion about clothes<br>• *Keep talking:* Different clothing items<br>• Discussion about good places to shop |
| **Interactions:**<br>Asking for a recommendation<br>Giving a recommendation | **Listening:**<br>Cities<br>At a tourist information desk<br>**Pronunciation:**<br>Word stress | **Reading:**<br>"Austin or San Antonio?"<br>A message board<br>**Writing:**<br>A message board | • Discussion about things to do in one day<br>• *Keep talking:* Discussion of possible things to do<br>• Role play at a tourist information desk<br>• Comparison of places in a town or a city<br>• *Keep talking:* City quiz<br>• Discussion about aspects of a city |
| **Interactions:**<br>Expressing certainty<br>Expressing uncertainty | **Listening:**<br>Friends playing a board game<br>People who made a difference<br>**Pronunciation:**<br>Simple past -*ed* endings | **Reading:**<br>"A Different Kind of Banker"<br>A biography<br>**Writing:**<br>A biography | • Guessing game about famous people<br>• *Keep talking:* Information gap activity about people from the past<br>• Guessing game about famous people<br>• Descriptions of admirable people<br>• *Keep talking:* Discussion about inspiring people<br>• Description of a person who made a difference |
| **Interactions:**<br>Ordering food<br>Checking information | **Listening:**<br>Customers ordering food<br>Restaurant impressions<br>**Pronunciation:**<br>*The* before vowel and consonant sounds | **Reading:**<br>"Restaurants with a Difference"<br>A webpage<br>**Writing:**<br>A review | • Discussion about eating out<br>• *Keep talking:* A menu<br>• Role play of a restaurant situation<br>• Discussion about food experiences<br>• *Keep talking:* Board game about food experiences<br>• Restaurant recommendations |
| **Interactions:**<br>Asking for suggestions<br>Giving a suggestion | **Listening:**<br>Fun things to do<br>An influential world musician<br>**Pronunciation:**<br>Reduction of *of* | **Reading:**<br>"African Superstars!"<br>A magazine article<br>**Writing:**<br>A popular musician | • Movie talk<br>• *Keep talking:* Movie favorites<br>• Suggestions about the weekend<br>• Class musical preferences<br>• *Keep talking:* Class survey about music<br>• A playlist |
| **Interactions:**<br>Reacting to bad news<br>Reacting to good news | **Listening:**<br>Sharing news<br>An interview with an athlete<br>**Pronunciation:**<br>Contraction of *will* | **Reading:**<br>"Students Raise Money for Baseball Team"<br>An article<br>**Writing:**<br>A dream come true | • Discussion about changes<br>• *Keep talking:* Reasons for doing things<br>• Good news and bad news<br>• Predictions about the future<br>• *Keep talking:* Predictions about next year<br>• Dream planner |

# Classroom language

**A** Write these actions below the correct pictures. Then compare with a partner.

| | | |
|---|---|---|
| Close your books. | Look at the picture. | Turn to page . . . |
| Listen. | ✓Open your books. | Work in groups. |
| Look at the board. | Raise your hand. | Work in pairs. |

1. *Open your books.*

2. _____

3. _____

4. _____

5. _____

6. _____

7. _____

8. _____

9. _____

**A:** *What's number one?*
**B:** *It's . . .*

**B** 🔊 Listen and check your answers.

**C** 🔊 Listen to seven of the actions. Do each one.

4

# Shopping

## Warm-up

1

2

3

4

5

6

**A** Describe the pictures. How many things can you name?

**B** Where do you usually shop? What do you like to buy?

## A  *It's lighter and thinner.*

## 1 Vocabulary  Opposites

**A** 🔊 Label the pictures with the correct words. Then listen and check your answers.

| big | expensive | heavy | loud | slow | thick |
|-----|-----------|-------|------|------|-------|

car

small     _big_

fan

quiet     _loud_

cell phone

thin     _thick_

computer

light     _heavy_

printer

fast     _slow_

camera   $49   $1,699

cheap     _expensive_

**B** **Pair work** Use the words in Part A to describe things you own. Tell your partner.

*"My cell phone is thin and light."*

## 2 Language in context  Which is better?

**A** 🔊 Read the message board. Then label the pictures.

**Star X07 or MyPhone?**

**michael12** Posted:     May 5  11:45 p.m.
Help! I need a phone and can't decide between the Star X07 and the MyPhone. Which is better?

**johnnyjay** Posted:     May 6  8:07 a.m.
Get the Star X07. It's lighter and thinner than the MyPhone.

**cybergal** Posted:     May 6  9:52 p.m.
The MyPhone is better. It's less expensive, and the Internet connection is faster. It has a larger choice of colors, too. The Star X07 comes only in black.

**B** Which of the two phones do you like?

## 3 Grammar 🔊 | **Comparative adjectives**

The Star X07 is **lighter than** the MyPhone.
The MyPhone is **heavier than** the Star X07.

Which cell phone is **more expensive**?
   The Star X07 is **more expensive than** the MyPhone.
   The MyPhone is **less expensive than** the Star X07.

Is the MyPhone **better than** the Star X07?
   No, I don't think it's **better**. It's **worse**.

| Adjective | Comparative |
| --- | --- |
| light | light**er** |
| nice | nice**r** |
| thin | thin**ner** |
| heavy | heav**ier** |
| difficult | **more / less** difficult |
| good | **better** |
| bad | **worse** |

Complete the sentences with the correct comparative form. Add *than* if necessary. Then compare with a partner.

1. Is your new printer _____ (fast) your old one?

2. Are desktop computers always _____ (heavy) laptops?

3. This new camera is really cheap! It's _____ (expensive) than my old one.

4. I like this TV, but I think I want a _____ (big) one.

5. This phone has an MP3 player, so it's _____ (expensive) other phones.

6. My new camera isn't _____ (good) my old one. In fact, it's _____ (bad)!

## 4 Speaking  Let's compare!

**A Pair work** Compare these products. How many sentences can you make?

Car A

Watch A

Camera A

Car B

Watch B

Camera B

**A:** *Car A is older than Car B.*
**B:** *And it's slower. Do you think Car A is quieter?*

**B Pair work** Which product in each pair do you prefer? Why?

## 5 Keep talking!

Go to page **139** for more practice.

I can describe and compare products. ☑

## 1 Interactions   Bargaining

**A** Do you ever bargain for lower prices? Where? For what? Do you enjoy bargaining?

**B** 🔊 Listen to the conversation. Does Eve buy the lamp?
Then practice the conversation.

**Eve:** Excuse me. How much is this lamp?
**Rob:** Oh, it's only $20.
**Eve:** Wow, that's expensive! How about $10?

**Rob:** No, I'm sorry. $20 is a good price.
**Eve:** Well, thanks anyway.
**Rob:** Wait! You can have it for $15.
**Eve:** $15? OK, I'll take it.

**C** 🔊 Listen to the expressions. Then practice the conversation again with the new expressions.

| Bargaining for a lower price | Suggesting a different price |
|---|---|
| How about . . . ?<br>Will you take . . . ?<br>Would you take . . . ? | You can have it / them for . . .<br>I'll let you have it / them for . . .<br>I'll give it / them to you for . . . |

**D** Number the sentences from 1 to 7. Then practice with a partner.

_____ **A:** *I'll take them! Thank you very much.*

_____ **A:** *$30? That's pretty expensive. Would you take $20?*

_____ **A:** *OK. Well, thank you anyway.*

_____ **A:** *Excuse me. How much are these earrings?*

_____ **B:** *Just a moment. I'll give them to you for $25.*

_____ **B:** *No, I'm sorry. $30 is the price.*

_____ **B:** *They're only $30.*

## 2 Pronunciation Linked sounds

**A** 🔊 Listen and repeat. Notice how final consonant sounds are often linked to the vowel sounds that follow them.

How mu**ch i**s this lamp?      It'**s o**nly $20.

**B** 🔊 Listen and mark the linked sounds. Then practice with a partner.

1. How much are the earrings?    2. Just a moment.    3. Thanks anyway.

## 3 Listening How much is it?

**A** 🔊 Listen to four people shopping at a yard sale. Number the pictures from 1 to 4. (There is one extra picture.)

☐   ☐   ☐   ☐   ☐

$ _____   $ _____   $ _____   $ _____   $ _____

**B** 🔊 Listen again. Write the price the buyer and seller agree on.

## 4 Speaking What a bargain!

**A** Write prices on the tags.

**B** **Pair work** Role-play the situations. Then change roles.

**Student A:** Sell the things. You want to sell them for a good price.
**Student B:** Buy the things. Bargain for lower prices.

A: *Excuse me. How much is the computer?*
B: *It's only $250.*
A: *That's very expensive! Would you take . . . ?*

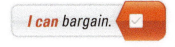

*I can* bargain. ☑

# C This hat is too small.

## 1 Vocabulary Adjectives to describe clothing

**A** 🔊 Complete the phrases with the correct words. Then listen and check your answers.

| baggy | comfortable | pretty | ugly |
|-------|-------------|--------|------|
| bright | plain | tight | uncomfortable |

1. a _____
shirt

2. _____
jeans

3. _____
shoes

4. a _____
blouse

5. a _____
tie

6. a _____
dress

7. _____
pants

8. an _____
hat

**B Pair work** Describe your clothing today. Tell your partner.

*"I think my shirt is plain, but comfortable. My jeans are a little baggy."*

## 2 Conversation Try it on!

**A** 🔊 Listen and practice.

**Allie:** Let's look at the jackets.
**Paul:** OK, but I have class at 3:00. Do we have enough time?
**Allie:** Sure. It's only 1:30. Hey! Look at this black one.
**Paul:** It's cool. Try it on.
**Allie:** OK. What do you think? Does it fit?
**Paul:** No, it's too small. Try this red one.
**Allie:** OK. How does it look? Is it big enough?
**Paul:** I think so. Yeah, it looks good on you.
**Allie:** How much is it? Can you see the tag?
**Paul:** Let's see . . . it's $120.
**Allie:** Oh, no! I only have $60. I don't have
enough money. I can't afford it!

**B** 🔊 Listen to the rest of the conversation. What else does Allie try on?

# 3 Grammar 🔊    *Enough* and *too*

**Enough** *means the right amount.* **Too** *means more than enough.*

| | | |
|---|---|---|
| Enough *before nouns* | Enough *after adjectives* | Too *before adjectives* |
| I have **enough** time. | The jacket is big **enough**. | The jacket is **too** small. |
| I don't have **enough** money. | The pants aren't long **enough**. | The pants aren't **too** long. |

**A** Complete the sentences with the correct words. Use *too* and *enough*. Then compare with a partner.

```
big   ✓long   money   uncomfortable
```

1. How do these pants look? Do you think they're  *long enough*  ?
2. These shoes look nice, but they're _____ . I can't walk at all.
3. Oh, no! I don't have _____ . This belt is $30, and I only have $20.
4. The shirt I ordered online is _____ . It fits very well.

**B** Rewrite the sentences. Use *enough* and *too*. Then compare with a partner.

1. Those boots are too small. (enough)      *These boots aren't big enough.*
2. That belt is $10. I have $10. (enough)      _____
3. The jacket is expensive. I can't afford it. (too)      _____
4. That belt is $12. I have $10. (enough)      _____
5. I wear a large size. This T-shirt isn't big enough. (too)      _____
6. These pants aren't long enough. (too)      _____

# 4 Speaking   Things I never wear

**A** Think about your closet at home. Complete the chart with pieces of clothing. Write reasons why you don't wear them.

| Things I don't like wearing | Things I never wear |
|---|---|
| *Ties – too ugly* | |
| | |
| | |
| | |

**B** **Group work** Share your ideas. What do you have in common?

# 5 Keep talking!

Student A go to page **140** and Student B go to page **144** for more practice.

**I can** describe how clothing looks and fits. ☑

# D A shopper's paradise

## 1 Reading 🔊

**A** Read the webpage. Which paragraph includes information about these topics?
Number the topics from 1 to 4.

☐ transportation    ☐ number of visitors    ☐ prices and money    ☐ hours

## CHATUCHAK WEEKEND MARKET

**1** With more than 15,000 shops and 200,000 visitors every Saturday and Sunday, Bangkok's Chatuchak Weekend Market is a popular place with visitors to Thailand. You can find plants, flowers, music, jewelry, clothes, food, and even animals!

**2** The market is a great place to find bargains, and prices are **generally** low. Most people bargain, but some don't, so don't worry if you don't want to bargain. Just go with a friendly smile and have enough cash in your pocket. There are ATMs for cash, but they are difficult to find, and many **vendors** don't take credit cards. The market is **huge**, and many people walk in circles, even with a map. Don't try to see it all in one day!

**3** The market is open from 8:00 to 6:00 Saturday and Sunday. It's good to get there early, before it gets too busy. Wear light, comfortable clothing and bring a bottle of water. And for lunch, try some of Thailand's famous snacks, such as fried scorpions!

**4** The market is very easy to get to. It's only a five-minute walk from Mo Chit station on Bangkok's Skytrain. Many people come by train but leave by taxi. It's easier to get your **purchases** back to your hotel that way!

**B** Read the webpage again. Find the words in **bold**, and check (✓) the correct meaning.

1. **generally** ☐ usually     3. **huge** ☐ easy to find
   ☐ rarely              ☐ very large

2. **vendors** ☐ buyers      4. **purchases** ☐ things you buy
   ☐ sellers             ☐ things you sell

**C** Check (✓) the tips you think the writer would agree with.

☐ Pay the first price the vendor offers.    ☐ Bring a credit card, not cash.
☐ Arrive in the morning.                    ☐ Take the bus home after shopping.

**D** **Pair work** What would you like about Bangkok's Weekend Market? What wouldn't you like? Tell your partner.

## 2 Listening  Portobello Road Market

**A** 🔊 Listen to two friends talk about Portobello Road Market. Answer the questions.

1. What city is the market in? _____
2. How many days is the outdoor market open? _____
3. When's a good time to visit? _____
4. What's a good way to get there? _____

**B** 🔊 Listen again. What can you buy at the market on Saturday? Circle the words you hear.

animals     cell phones     clothes     fruit     jewelry     meat     vegetables

## 3 Writing  An interesting market

**A** Think about a market you know. Answer the questions.

- What is the name of the market?
- Where is it?
- When is it open?
- When's a good time to visit?
- What can you buy there?

**B** Write a description of an interesting market. Use the model and your answers in Part A to help you.

> The Farmers' Market is near my home. It's open every Saturday from 9:00 to 4:00. You can buy the best fruit and vegetables there. A good time to visit is late in the afternoon. It's not too busy then. You don't bargain at this market, but sometimes vendors lower their prices at the end of the day.

**C Pair work**  Share your writing. How are the markets similar? How are they different?

## 4 Speaking  A good place to shop

**A** Think about things you buy. Add two more things to the list. Then complete the rest of the chart.

| Things I buy | Place | Reason |
|---|---|---|
| fruit and vegetables | | |
| shoes | | |
| old furniture | | |
| children's clothes | | |
| | | |
| | | |

**B Group work**  Share your ideas. Ask and answer questions for more information.

*"I always go to the market to buy fruit and vegetables. They are always fresh, and the people are friendly."*

**I can** discuss good places to shop. ☑

# Wrap-up

## 1 Quick pair review

**Lesson A** **Test your partner!** Say an adjective. Can your partner say its opposite? Take turns. You have one minute.

**A:** *Small.*
**B:** *Big.*

**Lesson B** **Do you remember?** Complete the conversation with the correct word. You have two minutes.

**A:** How much is this TV?

**B:** $50.

**A:** Will you _____ $30?
                      1

**B:** You can _____ it for $45.
                      2

**A:** How _____ $35?
                3

**B:** I'll _____ it to you for $40.
               4

**A:** OK.

**Lesson C** **Brainstorm!** Make a list of adjectives to describe clothing. Take turns. You and your partner have two minutes.

**Lesson D** **Find out!** What are two things both you and your partner buy at a market? Take turns. You and your partner have two minutes.

**A:** *I buy music at a market. Do you?*
**B:** *No, I don't. I buy music online.*

## 2 In the real world

What outdoor markets are famous? Go online and find information in English about an outdoor market. Then write about it.

- What's the name of the market?
- Where is it?
- When is it open?
- What do they sell at the market?

> *The Otavalo Market*
> *The Otavalo Market is in Ecuador.*
> *It's open every day, but Saturdays*
> *are very busy. . . .*

# Fun in the city

## Warm-up

1

2

3

4

5

6

**A** Describe the pictures. What is happening in each picture?

**B** Which of these things do you like about city life? Which don't you like?

# A  *You shouldn't miss it!*

## 1  Vocabulary  Places to see

**A** 🔊 Match the words and the pictures. Then listen and check your answers.

| | | | |
|---|---|---|---|
| a. botanical garden | c. fountain | e. palace | g. square |
| b. castle | d. monument | f. pyramid | h. statue |

1. ☐

2. ☐

3. ☐

4. ☐

5. ☐

6. ☐

7. ☐

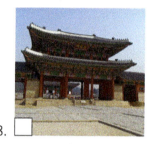
8. ☐

**B  Pair work** Which of the places in Part A do you have where you live? Discuss the places.

*"There's a nice statue in the center of the square."*

## 2  Language in context  Attractions in the city

**A** 🔊 Read about what to do in these three cities. Which cities are good for shopping?

### GUAYAQUIL, ECUADOR

Enjoy shopping, cafés, fountains, and statues on El Malecón, a popular walking area. It's a fantastic place to take a long, slow walk or ride on a tour boat.

### SEOUL, SOUTH KOREA

You shouldn't miss the small neighborhood of Insadong. It's a great place to shop for books, pottery, and paintings. Later, you can walk to a nearby palace or relax at an old teahouse.

### CAIRO, EGYPT

Love history? Then you should visit the Egyptian Museum. You can't see it all in one day, so be sure to see King Tut's treasure and the famous "mummy room."

**B** What about you? Which city in Part A would you like to visit? Why?

# 3 Grammar 🔊 *Should; can*

| *Should* for recommendations | *Can* for possibility |
|---|---|
| Where **should** I go? | What **can** I do there? |
| You **should** visit the Egyptian Museum. | You **can** enjoy cafés, shops, and fountains. |
| They **shouldn't** miss Insadong. | You **can't** see all of the museum in one day. |
| ( = They should see Insadong.) | |
| **Should** she go to Cairo? | **Can** they take a taxi? |
| Yes, she **should.**    No, she **shouldn't.** | Yes, they **can.**    No, they **can't.** |

Complete the conversation with *should, shouldn't, can,* or *can't.* Then practice with a partner.

**A:** ____*Should*____ I rent a car in Seoul?

**B:** No, I think you _____ take the subway. You _____ get around quickly and easily.

**A:** Oh, good. And what places _____ I visit?

**B:** Well, you _____ miss the palace, and you _____ also go to the art museum. You _____ see it all in one day because it's very big, but you _____ buy really nice art books and postcards there.

**A:** OK. Thanks a lot!

# 4 Listening My city

**A** 🔊 Listen to three people describe their cities. Number the pictures from 1 to 3.

Istanbul          Mexico City          Florence

1. _____   1. _____   1. _____
2. _____   2. _____   2. _____

**B** 🔊 Listen again. Write two things the people say visitors should do in their cities.

# 5 Speaking Only one day

**A Pair work** Imagine these people are planning to visit your town or city for only one day. What places should they visit?

- a family with teenage children
- a businessperson from overseas
- two college students
- young children on a school trip

*"I think the family should visit the town square. They can eat and shop there."*

**B Group work** Compare your answers from Part A. Do you agree?

# 6 Keep talking!

Go to page **142** for more practice.

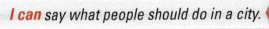

*I can say what people should do in a city.* ☑

# B I'd recommend going . . .

**A** Look at the pictures. What do you think the woman is going to do soon?

**B** 🔊 Listen to the conversation. Was your guess from Part A correct? Then practice the conversation.

**Lucy:** Hi, Alex.
**Alex:** Oh, hi, Lucy. Are you ready for your trip to Brazil?
**Lucy:** Almost, but I don't really know very much about Rio. What would you recommend doing there?

**Alex:** I'd recommend going to a samba club.
**Lucy:** A samba club? Really?
**Alex:** Yeah. You can dance or just listen to the music. Everyone has a good time.
**Lucy:** Great. That sounds fun!

**C** 🔊 Listen to the expressions. Then practice the conversation again with the new expressions.

| Asking for a recommendation | Giving a recommendation |
| --- | --- |
| What would you recommend doing there? <br> What would you suggest doing there? <br> What do you think I should do there? | I'd recommend going . . . <br> I'd suggest going . . . <br> I think you should go . . . |

**D** Put the words in order. Then compare with a partner.

1. you / there / recommend / what / seeing / would _____ ?
2. I'd / the castle / visiting / suggest _____ .
3. the square / I / should / think / you / go to _____ .
4. suggest / would / doing / what / you / in Tokyo _____ ?
5. bus / recommend / I'd / the / taking _____ .

## 2 Listening One day in Taipei

**A**  Listen to Carrie and David get information from the tourist information desk in Taipei. Check (✓) the recommendations you hear.

1. ☐ I'd suggest visiting Taipei 101.
   ☐ You should visit Taipei 101.
2. ☐ I'd recommend going to the night market.
   ☐ You shouldn't miss the night market.
3. ☐ I'd suggest going to the Fine Arts Museum.
   ☐ I'd recommend going to the Fine Arts Museum.
4. ☐ I think you should take the subway.
   ☐ I'd recommend taking the subway.

**B** 🔊 Listen again. Circle the recommendations in Part A that Carrie and David decide to follow.

## 3 Speaking Role play

**Pair work** Role-play the situation.
Then change roles.

**Student A:** You are a tourist in London. Ask for recommendations for three things to do.

**Student B:** You work at a tourist information desk. Give recommendations for three things to do.

### Top London Attractions

**The British Museum**
See the famous Rosetta Stone.

**The Tate Modern**
See great art for free.

**The London Eye**
Enjoy views of 55 famous places.

**Trafalgar Square**
Take your picture by the lion statues.

**Tower Bridge**
Walk across the bridge. Fantastic city views!

**Buckingham Palace**
See one of the Royal Family's many homes.

A: *Hello. Can I help you?*
B: *Yes. This is my first time in London. What would you suggest doing here?*
A: *Well, there are a lot of things to do, but I think you should definitely visit the British Museum. You can see . . .*

**I can** *ask for and give a recommendation.* ☑

# C The best and the worst

## 1 Vocabulary Adjectives to describe cities

**A** 🔊 Match the words and the pictures. Then listen and check your answers.

| a. beautiful | b. dangerous | c. dirty | d. modern | e. stressful |

1. ☐    2. ☐    3. ☐    4. ☐    5. ☐

**B** 🔊 Write the opposites. Use the words in Part A. Then listen and check your answers.

| clean | relaxing | safe | traditional | ugly |
| --- | --- | --- | --- | --- |
| _dirty_ | _____ | _____ | _____ | _____ |

**C** Pair work Describe where you live using the words in Parts A and B.

*"Our city is beautiful and clean, but life here can be stressful."*

## 2 Conversation Life in Sydney

**A** 🔊 Listen and practice.

**Peter:** So, Akemi, how do you like living in Sydney?

**Akemi:** I miss Japan sometimes, but I love it here. I think it's the most beautiful and one of the most exciting cities in the world.

**Peter:** But do you find it stressful?

**Akemi:** Not at all. I know Sydney is the biggest city in Australia, but remember, I'm from Tokyo.

**Peter:** Oh, yeah. What else do you like about living here?

**Akemi:** A lot of things. It's very clean and safe. The people are friendly. Oh, and the food here is fantastic.

**Peter:** I agree. I think Sydney has the best restaurants in the country.

**Akemi:** Hey, do you want to get something to eat?

**Peter:** Sure. I know a nice café. It's cheap but good.

**B** 🔊 Listen to their conversation in the café. How does Akemi describe the café? How does Peter describe the food?

# 3 Grammar 🔊 | Superlative adjectives

Sydney is **the biggest** city in Australia.
Sydney is one of **the most exciting** cities in the world.
Sydney has **the best** restaurants in the country.

What's **the cleanest** city in your country?
What city has **the most traditional** restaurants?
Is it **the worst** restaurant?
    Yes, it is.    No, it isn't.

| Adjective | Superlative |
|-----------|-------------|
| clean | **the** clean**est** |
| safe | **the** safe**st** |
| big | **the** big**gest** |
| ugly | **the** ugl**iest** |
| stressful | **the most** stressful |
| good | **the best** |
| bad | **the worst** |

**A** Complete the questions with the superlative form of the adjectives. Then compare
with a partner.

1. What's one of _____ (old) universities
   in your country?
2. What's _____ (big) city in your country?
3. What's _____ (modern) city in your country?
4. What's _____ (beautiful) national park?
5. What city has _____ (good) restaurants?
6. What city has _____ (bad) weather?

University of Cambridge

**B** Ask and answer the questions in Part A. Discuss your ideas.

# 4 Pronunciation  Word stress

**A** 🔊 Listen and repeat. Notice the stress in the names of these cities.

| ● ·     | · ●    | ● · ·    | · ● ·     |
|---------|--------|----------|-----------|
| **Syd**ney | Ma**drid** | **Can**berra | New **Del**hi |
|         |        |          |           |

**B** 🔊 Listen and write the cities in the correct columns in Part A. Then practice
with a partner.

Amsterdam    Berlin    Caracas    Lima

# 5 Speaking  What's the . . . ?

**Pair work** Ask and answer questions about your town or city.

| expensive / hotel | exciting / neighborhood | modern / building |
|-------------------|-------------------------|-------------------|
| beautiful / park | big / department store | relaxing / place |

**A:** *What's the most expensive hotel?*
**B:** *I'm not sure it's the most expensive, but the Grand Hotel is very expensive.*

# 6 Keep talking!

Go to page **143** for more practice.

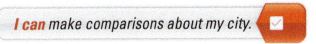
*I can* make comparisons about my city.

# D The best place to go

## 1 Reading 🔊

**A** Read the message board. Who answers Miguel's question about safety?

### Austin or San Antonio?

**miguel** Posted: *May 17 7:06 p.m.*

Hi! I live in Mexico and am planning to visit my uncle in Dallas, Texas, next year. I'd also like to visit Austin or San Antonio for a few days. I like the outdoors, local music, good food, friendly people, etc. Are both cities safe? Any other tips appreciated. Thanks! Miguel

**rocker** Posted: *May 17 7:23 p.m.*

I'm a musician and live in Austin. I think the music here is the best in Texas. In fact, Austin's nickname is "the Live Music Capital of the World." I can send you the names of some cool music clubs. We have fantastic restaurants here, too.

**biker68** Posted: *May 17 8:54 p.m.*

Definitely visit San Antonio. The River Walk is one of the most popular things for visitors to do. There's a lot to do outdoors here, too. And everyone in Texas is very friendly. Check out my pics: **myphotos**

**susanp** Posted: *May 17 11:09 p.m.*

I disagree with rocker. I think the music is better in San Antonio. I lived in both cities. There is a lot to do outdoors in San Antonio, but there's just more to do in Austin.

**richard** Posted: *May 18 6:45 a.m.*

Both cities are safe, by the way, so don't worry. I live in Houston. It's the largest city in Texas. You should visit here, too. 🙂 Read my travel blog at **richard23.cup.org**.

**traveler** Posted: *May 18 10:31 a.m.*

San Antonio has the best food in Texas. Do you like Tex-Mex food? You should go in spring or fall (summer is hot!). I suggest traveling by bus. It's not expensive. Email me with any questions.

**miguel** Posted: *May 18 3:22 p.m.*

Miguel here again. Thanks, everyone!

**B** Read the message board again. Answer the questions. Check (✓) your answers.

| Who . . . ? | rocker | biker68 | susanp | richard | traveler |
|---|---|---|---|---|---|
| lives in Houston | ☐ | ☐ | ☐ | ☐ | ☐ |
| gives a link to see pictures | ☐ | ☐ | ☐ | ☐ | ☐ |
| writes about the weather | ☐ | ☐ | ☐ | ☐ | ☐ |
| prefers the music in San Antonio | ☐ | ☐ | ☐ | ☐ | ☐ |
| has a travel blog | ☐ | ☐ | ☐ | ☐ | ☐ |
| is a musician | ☐ | ☐ | ☐ | ☐ | ☐ |

**C Pair work** What do you do when you need advice or a recommendation? Who do you talk to? Tell your partner.

## **2** Writing A message board

**A** Choose a topic for a message board. Then write a question asking for a recommendation about your topic. Use the model to help you.

- food
- music
- outdoor activities
- transportation

**B** **Group work** Pass your question to the classmate on your right. Read and answer your classmate's question. Continue to pass, read, and answer all of the questions in your group.

**C** Read the answers to your question. Which recommendation is the best?

> *Can you suggest a good restaurant near our school?*
>
> 1. *You should go to Mickey's. It's fantastic, but it's expensive.*
> 2. *I think Thai Palace has the best food.*
> 3. *I agree. It's the most popular restaurant near here.*

## **3** Speaking The best of the city

**A** **Pair work** Complete the chart with information about the best things about your city or town. Give reasons.

| The best things about _____ | Reasons |
|---|---|
|  |  |
|  |  |
|  |  |
|  |  |
|  |  |

**A:** *I think the best thing about our city is the people. They are very friendly and helpful.*
**B:** *I agree.*

**B** **Group work** Compare your ideas with another pair. Do you agree?

**C** **Class activity** Make a list of all the things from Parts A and B. Which is the most popular?

I can *discuss aspects of a city.* ☑

# Wrap-up

## 1 Quick pair review

**Lesson A** **Brainstorm!** Make a list of fun places to see in a city. How many do you know? You have one minute.

**Lesson B** **Do you remember?** Check (✓) the questions you can ask when you want a recommendation. You have one minute.

☐ What would you recommend doing there?

☐ Which place is more expensive?

☐ When are you going to China?

☐ What would you suggest doing there?

☐ What are you going to do in Brazil?

☐ What do you think I should do there?

**Lesson C** **Test your partner!** Say an adjective to describe a city. Can your partner say the superlative? Take turns. You have one minute.

**A:** *Modern.*
**B:** *The most modern.*

**Lesson D** **Guess!** Describe a city, but don't say its name. Can your partner guess what it is? Take turns. You and your partner have two minutes.

**A:** *It's an old city in Europe. It's beautiful. It has a lot of squares and fountains.*
**B:** *Is it Florence?*
**A:** *Yes, it is.*

## 2 In the real world

What city would you like to visit? Go to a travel website and find information about the city in English. Then write about it.

- What country is it in?
- What's it like?
- What is there to do in the city?
- What's it famous for?

> *Montreal*
> *I would like to go to Montreal. It's in Canada. It's modern and safe. . . .*

# People

| LESSON **A** | LESSON **B** | LESSON **C** | LESSON **D** |
|---|---|---|---|
| • Careers<br>• *Was / Were born*; past of *be* | • Expressing certainty<br>• Expressing uncertainty | • Personality adjectives<br>• Simple past; *ago* | • Reading: "A Different Kind of Banker"<br>• Writing: A biography |

## Warm-up

1. ☐
2. ☐
3. ☐
4. ☐
5. ☐
6. ☐

a
b
c
d
e
f

**A** Match the people and the things they are famous for. Check your answers on page 94.

**B** Which of the people in Part A would you like to meet? Why?

# A  *Where was he born?*

## 1 Vocabulary  Careers

**A** 🔊 Match the words and the pictures. Then listen and check your answers.

| | | | |
|---|---|---|---|
| a. astronaut | c. composer | e. director | g. politician |
| b. athlete | d. designer | f. explorer | h. scientist |

 1. ☐

 2. ☐

 3. ☐

 4. ☐

 5. ☐

 6. ☐

 7. ☐

 8. ☐

**B** **Pair work**  Give an example of a famous person for each category.

*"Ang Lee is a famous director."*

## 2 Language in context  Famous firsts

**A** 🔊 Read about these famous firsts. Which famous first happened first?

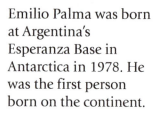

Emilio Palma was born at Argentina's Esperanza Base in Antarctica in 1978. He was the first person born on the continent.

The first person on the moon in 1969 was American astronaut Neil Armstrong. He was on the moon for only two and a half hours.

Junko Tabei was the first woman to climb Mt. Everest in 1975. She was also the first woman to climb the highest mountains on all seven continents.

Venus and Serena Williams are great athletes. They were the first sisters to win Wimbledon in 2000.

**B**  Which people from Part A would you like to meet? What question would you ask them?

## 3 Grammar 🔊 | *Was / Were born;* past of *be*

| | |
|---|---|
| Where **was** Emilio Palma **born**?<br>  He **was born** in Antarctica.<br>  He **wasn't born** in Argentina. | How long **was** Neil Armstrong on the moon?<br>  He **was** there for two and a half hours.<br>  He **wasn't** there for very long. |
| Where **were** Venus and Serena **born**?<br>  They **were born** in the U.S.<br>  They **weren't born** in Canada. | Where **were** his parents from?<br>  They **were** from Argentina.<br>  They **weren't** from Antarctica. |
| **Was** he **born** in Antarctica?<br>  Yes, he **was**.     No, he **wasn't**. | **Were** they Wimbledon champions in 2000?<br>  Yes, they **were**.     No, they **weren't**. |

**A** Complete these sentences with the correct past form of *be*.
Then compare with a partner.

1. Coco Chanel _____ an amazing French designer.
2. Albert Einstein _____ born in Germany.
3. Alfred Hitchcock _____ a great director.
4. Diego Rivera and Frida Kahlo _____ born in Mexico.
5. Mozart and Beethoven _____ famous composers.

**B** Correct the false sentences. Then compare with a partner.

1. Ronald Reagan was a British politician. (American)
   *He wasn't a British politician. He was an American politician.*
2. Zheng He was an early Chinese scientist. (explorer)
   _____
3. Artist Vincent van Gogh was born in the 20th century. (19th century)
   _____
4. Gianni Versace and Yves Saint Laurent were explorers. (designers)
   _____
5. Venus and Serena Williams were born in the late 1970s. (early 1980s)
   _____

## 4 Speaking Famous people

**Group work** Choose a person from the past. Your group asks
questions and guesses the person's name. Take turns.

**A:** *He was from Mexico. He was a politician.*
**B:** *Is it . . . ?*
**A:** *No, sorry. He was born in the 19th century.*
**C:** *I think I know. Is it Benito Juárez?*

## 5 Keep talking!

Student A go to page 141 and Student B go to page 145 for more practice.

> *I can* ask and talk about people from the past. ☑

# *I'm not sure, but I think . . .*

## **1** Interactions    Certainty and uncertainty

**A** Look at the pictures. Where are the people? What are they doing?

**B** 🔊 Listen to the conversation. Does Mike know the answers to both questions? Then practice the conversation.

**Mike:** Let's go over more questions before our test tomorrow.
**Jenny:** OK. What was the original name of New York City?
**Mike:** It was New Amsterdam.
**Jenny:** Are you sure?
**Mike:** I'm positive.

**Jenny:** Correct! This one's more difficult. Who was Plato's teacher?
**Mike:** I'm not sure, but I think it was Aristotle.
**Jenny:** Actually, Aristotle was Plato's student. Socrates was his teacher.
**Mike:** Oh, right.

**C** 🔊 Listen to the expressions. Then practice the conversation again with the new expressions.

| Expressing certainty | Expressing uncertainty |
|---|---|
| I'm positive.<br>I'm certain.<br>I'm sure. | I'm not sure, but I think . . .<br>I'm not certain, but I think . . .<br>I'm not positive, but I think . . . |

**D** Circle the answer you think is correct. Practice with a partner and use expressions from Part C. Then check your answers on page 94.

1. Bill Clinton was president of the **U.S. / U.K.**

2. Mozart was born in the **16th / 17th / 18th** century.

3. David Beckham's first soccer team was **Manchester United / Real Madrid.**

4. Che Guevara was born in **Bolivia / Argentina / Cuba.**

5. The 2008 Olympics were in **Sydney / Athens / Beijing.**

**A:** *Bill Clinton was president of the U.S.*
**B:** *Are you sure?*
**A:** *I'm positive.*

## 2 Listening Sorry, that's not right.

**A** Do you know the answers to these questions? Write your guesses in the first column.

| | | Your guess | Player's guess | |
|---|---|---|---|---|
| 1. | Where were the 2000 Olympics? | | | ☐ |
| 2. | Who was the winner of the 2006 World Cup? | | | ☐ |
| 3. | In what century was Pablo Picasso born? | | | ☐ |
| 4. | Who was the author of the play *Hamlet?* | | | ☐ |
| 5. | How long was Bill Clinton president of the U.S.? | | | ☐ |

**B** 🔊 Listen to four friends play a board game. Write the players' guesses in the second column.

**C** 🔊 Listen again. Check (✓) the players' guesses that are correct.

## 3 Speaking Do you know?

**A Pair work** Look at the pictures and the categories. Add another category. Then write two questions for each category. Be sure you know the answers!

Actors and actresses

_____

_____

Athletes

_____

_____

Singers and musicians

_____

_____

_____

_____

_____

**B Group work** Ask your questions. Use expressions of certainty or uncertainty in the answers.

A: *Where was Brad Pitt born?*
B: *I'm not sure, but I think he was born in . . .*
A: *How old is he?*

> **I can** express certainty and uncertainty. ✓

## C People I admire

### 1 Vocabulary Personality adjectives

**A** 🔊 Match the words in the paragraphs and the definitions. Then listen and check your answers.

I admire U.S. President Abraham Lincoln. He was **honest**[1] as a lawyer and often worked for free. He was **brave**[2] and kept the country together during war. He was a very **inspiring**[3] person.

— Jin Ju

Nobel Peace Prize winner Dr. Wangari Maathai is very **passionate**[4] about her environmental work. She's very **intelligent**,[5] and I really admire her.

— Celia

Bono is a **talented**[6] musician, but he's also a **caring**[7] person. I admire him for his fight against world poverty. He's very **determined**,[8] and he's helping a lot of poor people.

— Mark

| _____ very good at something | _____ making other people want to do something |
| _1_ open, telling the truth | _____ able to understand things quickly and easily |
| _____ not afraid of anything | _____ trying everything possible to do something |
| _____ nice to other people | _____ showing a strong feeling about something |

**B Pair work** What other personality adjectives can you think of? Discuss your ideas.

### 2 Conversation I really admire him.

**A** 🔊 Listen and practice.

**Paul:** Did you finish your report, Emma?

**Emma:** Yeah, I did. I finished it two days ago.

**Paul:** Good for you! So who did you write about?

**Emma:** Jacques Cousteau. I really admire him.

**Paul:** I don't think I know him. What did he do?

**Emma:** A lot! He was a French scientist and explorer. He loved nature and studied the sea. He made documentaries and wrote books about the world's oceans. He won a lot of prizes for his work.

**Paul:** Wow! He sounds like an inspiring guy.

**Emma:** He was. He was really passionate about his work.

**B** 🔊 Listen to the rest of the conversation. When did Jacques Cousteau die?

# 3 Grammar 🔊 | Simple past; *ago*

| | |
|---|---|
| Who **did** you **write** about?<br>　I **wrote** about Jacques Cousteau.<br>　I **didn't write** about his son.<br>What **did** he **do**?<br>　He **made** documentaries.<br>**Did** you **finish** your report?<br>　Yes, I **did**.　No, I **didn't**. | **Period of time + *ago***<br>I finished the report **two days ago**.<br>I researched it **a week ago**.<br>I saw a documentary **four years ago**.<br>He died **a long time ago**. |

**A** Complete the conversation with the simple past form of the verbs. Then practice with a partner.

**A:** Why _____ you _____ (decide) to write about Mia Hamm for your report?

**B:** Well, I _____ (want) to write about an athlete. And I think she's very inspiring. In 1997, she _____ (start) the Mia Hamm Foundation. It helps women in sports. Then in 2000, she _____ (write) the book *Go for the Goal*.

**A:** Does she play soccer now?

**B:** No, she _____ (play) her last game in 2004, and then in 2007 she _____ (have) twin girls!

**B** **Pair work** Ask and answer questions about when Mia Hamm did these things. Use *ago* in the answers.

| | | | |
|---|---|---|---|
| have twins | play her last game | start a foundation | write a book |

# 4 Pronunciation Simple past -*ed* endings

🔊 Listen and repeat. Notice the different ways the simple past endings are pronounced.

| /t/ | | /d/ | | /ɪd/ | |
|---|---|---|---|---|---|
| finished | asked | played | admired | wanted | created |

# 5 Speaking What did they do?

**Group work** Use the adjectives to describe people you know. What did the people do?

| | | | | |
|---|---|---|---|---|
| brave | caring | honest | intelligent | talented |

*"My sister Megumi is very brave. She traveled alone in Canada and . . ."*

# 6 Keep talking!

Go to page 146 for more practice.

| I can describe people I admire. ☑ |
|---|

# D Making a difference

## 1 Reading ◄))

**A** Read the biography. How did Dr. Muhammad Yunus make a difference?

a. He won the Nobel Peace Prize.     b. He helped the poor.     c. He studied economics.

### A DIFFERENT KIND OF BANKER

Dr. Muhammad Yunus, a banker and economist, was born in Bangladesh in 1940. He studied economics at Dhaka University in Bangladesh. He taught for a few years and then went to the United States to continue his studies. He returned home to Bangladesh in 1972 and started teaching again.

One day in 1976, Yunus visited a poor **village** in his home country. There he met some women who wanted to make furniture, but they didn't have enough money. He decided to help them and gave them $27 of his own money. They made and sold the furniture, **made a profit**, and then returned the money to Dr. Yunus. At that point, he saw how very little money could help a lot. He decided to help poor people. A bank **loaned** him the money.

In 1983, Yunus started the Grameen Bank. This bank loans money to poor people. Dr. Yunus and Grameen Bank received the 2006 Nobel Peace Prize for their work with the poor.

In 2009, the bank had 7.95 million customers, and 97% of these customers were women. The success of the bank inspired other people in many different countries to start similar banks. Yunus once said, "**Conventional** banks look for the rich; we look for the absolutely poor."

**B** Number these events from Dr. Yunus's life from 1 to 8.

_____ He returned to Bangladesh.          _____ He studied at Dhaka University.

_____ He was born in 1940.               _____ He gave money to some women in 1976.

_____ He started the Grameen Bank.        _____ He won the Nobel Peace Prize.

_____ He studied in the United States.    _____ He inspired other people.

**C** Read the biography again. Find the words in **bold**, and check (✓) the correct meaning.

1. A **village** is:

   ☐ a very small town          ☐ a big place where a lot of people live

2. If you **made a profit**, you:

   ☐ lost money                 ☐ made money

3. If someone **loaned** you money, you:

   ☐ gave back the money        ☐ kept the money

4. A **conventional** bank is:

   ☐ usual                      ☐ unusual

**D** **Pair work** How would you describe Dr. Yunus? Tell your partner.

## 2 Writing  A biography

**A Pair work** Discuss famous people who made a big difference in people's lives. Answer the questions.

- What are their names?
- What do you know about their lives?
- What did they do?
- How did they make a difference?

**B** Write a short biography about a famous person who made a difference. Use the model and your answers in Part A to help you.

*José Antonio Abreu*
*José Antonio Abreu is a Venezuelan economist. He is also a talented musician. In 1975, he started a music school for poor children. He wanted to help these children and was determined to change their lives with music. Today, children all over Venezuela are playing in orchestras.*

**C Group work** Share your writing. Who do you think made the biggest difference?

## 3 Listening  Life lessons

**A** 🔊 Listen to three people describe the people who made a difference in their lives. Check (✓) the qualities they use to describe those people.

| | Qualities | | What did the people teach them? |
|---|---|---|---|
| 1. | ☐ caring <br> ☐ talented | ☐ intelligent <br> ☐ creative | a. how to sing <br> b. to be a musician |
| 2. | ☐ brave <br> ☐ honest | ☐ generous <br> ☐ determined | a. never to quit <br> b. how to play soccer |
| 3. | ☐ determined <br> ☐ caring | ☐ honest <br> ☐ inspiring | a. how to teach English <br> b. the qualities of a good teacher |

**B** 🔊 Listen again. What did the people teach them? Circle the correct answers.

## 4 Speaking  In my life

**Group work** Tell your group about a person who made a difference in your life. Use the questions below and your own ideas.

- How do you know this person?
- What did he or she teach you?
- What did he or she do?
- How would you describe him or her?

**A:** *My aunt made a big difference in my life.*
**B:** *Oh, yeah? Why?*
**A:** *She taught me to think of other people.*

*I can describe people who made a difference.*

# Wrap-up

## 1 Quick pair review

**Lesson A** **Brainstorm!** Make a list of careers. How many do you know? You have two minutes.

**Lesson B** **Guess!** Say the name of a famous person. Does your partner know where he or she was born? Take turns. You have two minutes.

**A:** *Albert Einstein.*
**B:** *He was born in Germany.*
**A:** *Are you sure?*
**B:** *I'm positive.*

**B:** *Michelle Obama.*
**A:** *I'm not certain, but I think she was born in Chicago.*

**Lesson C** **Test your partner!** Say six verbs. Can your partner write the simple past forms of the verbs correctly? Check his or her answers. Take turns. You and your partner have two minutes.

1. _____   3. _____   5. _____
2. _____   4. _____   6. _____

**Lesson D** **Find out!** Who are two people both you and your partner think made a difference in the world? What qualities do they have? Take turns. You and your partner have two minutes.

**A:** *I think Nelson Mandela made a difference.*
**B:** *Me, too. He's determined and inspiring.*
**A:** *Yes, he is.*

## 2 In the real world

Who do you admire? Go online and find five things he or she did that you think are interesting. Then write about this person.

> *Roger Federer*
> *I admire Roger Federer. He's a great tennis player. He also helps a lot of poor people. . . .*

Answers to Interactions, Part D (page 88)
1. U.S.  2. 18th  3. Manchester United  4. Argentina  5. Beijing

Answers to Warm-up, Part A (page 85)
1. e  2. f  3. b  4. c  5. d  6. a

94

# In a restaurant

**LESSON A**
- Menu items
- Articles

**LESSON B**
- Ordering food
- Checking information

**LESSON C**
- Interesting food
- Present perfect for experience

**LESSON D**
- Reading: "Restaurants with a Difference"
- Writing: A review

## Warm-up

1. ☐

2. ☐

3. ☐

4. ☐

5. ☐

6. ☐

**A** What kinds of food do you think each place serves?

**B** Check (✓) the top three places you would like to try. Why?

# A  *The ice cream is fantastic!*

## 1 Vocabulary  Menu items

**A** 🔊 Label the menu with the correct words. Then listen and check your answers.

| Appetizers | Desserts | Main dishes | Side dishes |

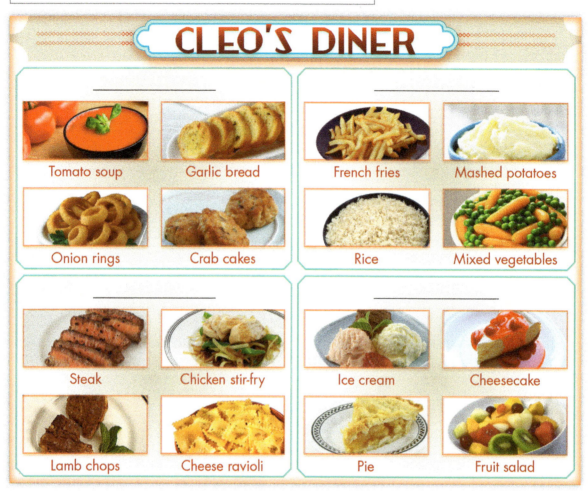

### CLEO'S DINER

_____

Tomato soup     Garlic bread

Onion rings     Crab cakes

_____

French fries     Mashed potatoes

Rice     Mixed vegetables

_____

Steak     Chicken stir-fry

Lamb chops     Cheese ravioli

_____

Ice cream     Cheesecake

Pie     Fruit salad

**B Pair work**  Give an example of another menu item for each category.

*"Another example of a main dish is spaghetti and meatballs. Another side dish . . ."*

## 2 Language in context  Any recommendations?

**A** 🔊 Listen to Jeff chat with his friends online. Who recommends the ice cream?

**jeff:**  I'm thinking of eating out tonight. Any recommendations?
**junko:**  I'd recommend going to Cleo's Diner. They have great food and good service.
**tony12:**  Yeah, Cleo's is amazing. Get an appetizer there. They're excellent.
**jeff:**  GR8! How are the main dishes?
**tony12:**  I had a steak with some French fries. The steak was great, but the fries weren't.
**junko:**  You should try a dessert there, too. The ice cream is fantastic!
**jeff:**  I love ice cream!! THX. 🙂 Does anyone want to join me?

**B**  What about you? What do you do when you need a recommendation for a restaurant?

# 3 Grammar 🔊 Articles

| | |
|---|---|
| *Use* a / an *to talk about nonspecific singular count nouns.*<br><br>    Try **a** dessert.<br>    Get **an** appetizer.<br><br>*Use* some *before plural count and noncount nouns.*<br><br>    Let's order **some** French fries.<br>    Let's order **some** garlic bread. | *Use* the *to talk about specific count and noncount nouns.*<br><br>    I had **the** crab cakes.<br>    **The** ice cream is fantastic.<br><br>*Use* the *to name count and noncount nouns a second time.*<br><br>    I had a steak and some French fries.<br>    **The** steak was great, but **the** fries weren't. |

Circle the correct words. Then compare with a partner.

**A:** I'm glad we came here. It's a great place.
**B:** So, do you want to share **an** / **some** appetizer?
**A:** Sure. How about **an** / **the** onion rings?
**B:** Perfect!
**A:** And do you want to get **a** / **some** crab cakes?
**B:** I don't think so. I'm not *that* hungry.
**A:** I'm going to get **a** / **the** lamb chops with **a** / **some** rice.
**B:** I think I want **a** / **the** steak. I heard it's delicious.
**A:** **A** / **The** desserts are good. I love **an** / **the** ice cream.
**B:** Yeah, we should order **a** / **an** dessert later.
**A:** Let's find **the** / **some** waiter. Where is he?

# 4 Pronunciation *The* before vowel and consonant sounds

**A** 🔊 Listen and repeat. Notice how *the* is pronounced before vowel and consonant sounds.

| /i/ | | | /ə/ | | |
|---|---|---|---|---|---|
| the **a**ppetizer | the **i**ce cream | the **o**range | the lamb | the fruit | the pie |

**B Pair work** Practice the conversation in Exercise 3.

# 5 Speaking What to order?

**A Pair work** Do you usually order an appetizer, a main dish, a side dish, and a dessert in restaurants? Discuss your ideas.

    **A:** *I usually order a main dish and a side dish. I don't really like desserts.*
    **B:** *I sometimes order an appetizer, but I always order a dessert.*

**B Pair work** Look back at the menu in Exercise 1. What would you order?

*"The chicken stir-fry and the rice look good. I'd order that."*

# 6 Keep talking!

Go to page 147 for more practice.

I **can** talk about menus and eating out. ☑

# B  I'll have the fish, please.

## 1 Interactions    At a restaurant

**A** When was the last time you went to a restaurant? Who did you go with? What did you order?

**B** 🔊 Listen to the conversation. What does Maria order? Then practice the conversation.

**Waiter:** Are you ready to order?
**Maria:** Yes, I think so.
**Waiter:** What would you like?
**Maria:** I'll have the fish with some rice, and a small salad, please.
**Waiter:** Anything else?

**Maria:** No, I don't think so.
**Waiter:** All right. Let me check that.
You'd like the fish, with rice, and a small salad.
**Maria:** Yes, that's right.
**Waiter:** Would you like some water?
**Maria:** Sure, that would be great. Thank you.

**C** 🔊 Listen to the expressions. Then practice the conversation again with the new expressions.

| Ordering food |
|---|
| I'll have . . . , please. |
| I'd like . . . , please. |
| Can I have . . . , please? |

| Checking information |
|---|
| Let me check that. |
| Let me read that back. |
| Let me repeat that. |

**D** **Pair work** Have conversations like the one in Part B. Use the food below.

## **2** Listening Food orders

**A** 🔊 Listen to people order food. How many people order dessert?
Circle the correct answer.

one      two      three

**B** 🔊 Listen again. Correct any wrong information on these orders.

1.

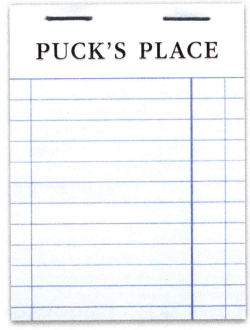

*Mickey's*

| chicken | | |
| rice | | |
| mixed vegetables | | |
| apple pie | | |

2.

*Mickey's*

| crab cakes | | |
| lamb chops | | |
| French fries | | |
| small salad | | |
| water | | |
| chocolate cake | | |
| medium mushroom pizza | | |
| iced tea | | |

## **3** Speaking Role play

**Pair work** Role-play the situation. Then change roles.

**Student A:** You are a waiter or a waitress at Puck's Place. Greet the customer, take his
or her order, and then check the information.

**Student B:** You are a customer at Puck's Place. Order from the menu.

**PUCK'S PLACE**

### PUCK'S PLACE

**Appetizers**
Chicken salad • Pasta salad • Onion soup
Chicken soup • Crab cakes • Garlic bread

**Main dishes**
Lamb chops • Steak
Chicken stir-fry • Fish • Cheese ravioli

**Sides**
French fries • Rice
Mixed vegetables • Mashed potatoes

**Desserts**
Apple pie • Chocolate ice cream • Fruit salad

**Drinks**
Tea • Coffee • Lemonade • Soda

**A:** *Hello. Are you ready to order?*
**B:** *Yes. I'll have the onion soup. And can I have the*
*fish and some white rice, please? Also, . . .*

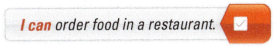

**I can** order food in a restaurant. ☑

# C Have you ever...?

## 1 Vocabulary  Interesting food

**A** 🔊 Complete the chart with the correct words. Then listen and check your answers.

avocados     blue cheese     carrot juice     dates     frozen yogurt

oysters     plantains     seaweed     soy milk     squid

| Dairy | Seafood | Fruit / Vegetables | Drinks |
| --- | --- | --- | --- |
|  |  |  |  |
|  |  |  |  |
|  |  |  |  |
|  |  |  |  |

**B** **Pair work**  Which food in Part A do you like? do you dislike? would you like to try? Tell your partner.

*"I like oysters. I don't like carrot juice. I'd like to try squid."*

## 2 Conversation  Dinner plans

**A** 🔊 Listen and practice.

**Ellen:** What are you doing tonight?
**Peter:** I'm going to World Café with my brother. Have you ever been there?
**Ellen:** No, I haven't. But I heard it's good.
**Peter:** I looked at their menu online this morning. They serve some really interesting food.
**Ellen:** Oh, yeah? Like what?
**Peter:** Fresh oysters. I've never had oysters, so I want to try them. Have you ever eaten them?
**Ellen:** Yeah, I have. I think they're delicious.
**Peter:** I've had squid. Are they similar?
**Ellen:** Um, not really. Do they only serve seafood?
**Peter:** No, they serve a little of everything.

**B** 🔊 Listen to Peter's message to Ellen the next day. What food did he like?

# 3 Grammar 🔊 Present perfect for experience

| | | |
|---|---|---|
| I've **been** to World Café. | I **haven't tried** the desserts. | **Past participles** |
| I've **had** squid. | I've never **eaten** oysters. | be **been** |
| | | drink **drunk** |
| **Have** you **ever been** to World Café? | | eat **eaten** |
| Yes, I **have**. No, I **haven't**. | | have **had** |
| | | try **tried** |
| *Contractions* I've = I have I haven't = I have not | | |

**A** Complete the conversation with the present perfect form of the verbs. Then practice with a partner.

1. **A:** This place looks fun. I _____ (never / be) here.

   **B:** I love it here. I _____ (be) here many times.

   **A:** Everything looks delicious.

   **B:** _____ you _____ (ever / eat) Mexican food before?

   **A:** I _____ (have) tacos, but I'd like to try something new.

2. **A:** I _____ (never / try) frozen yogurt. Can you recommend a flavor?

   **B:** I _____ (have) most flavors, and they're all good.

   **A:** _____ you _____ (ever / try) the green tea flavor?

   **B:** No, I _____ (have / not), but you should try it!

**B** Make sentences about your food experiences.

1. be / to a Turkish restaurant _____
2. eat / oysters _____
3. drink / soy milk _____
4. have / plantains _____
5. try / blue cheese _____

**C** **Pair work** Ask *Have you ever . . . ?* questions about the experiences in Part B.

# 4 Speaking Food experiences

**A** Add two more food experiences to the list.

| eat / dates | have / seaweed | _____ / _____ |
|---|---|---|
| try / Vietnamese food | drink / carrot juice | _____ / _____ |

**B** **Pair work** Discuss your experiences. What food would you like to try?

**A:** *Have you ever tried Vietnamese food?*
**B:** *Yes, I have. It's delicious!*

# 5 Keep talking!

Go to page 148 for more practice.

I **can** ask about and describe food experiences. ✓

# D Restaurant experiences

## 1 Reading 🔊

**A** Read the webpage. Which sentence describes all three restaurants? Check (✓) the correct answer.

- ☐ They don't have a lot of light.
- ☐ They're not very expensive.
- ☐ They are in good locations.
- ☐ They are very unusual.

★ **RESTAURANTS WITH A DIFFERENCE** ★

Ninja Akasaka is a popular restaurant in Tokyo. A ninja in dark clothes greets guests at the door and takes them through the dark hallways of the ninja house to their tables. The waiters also dress as ninjas. Ninja Akasaka has over a hundred delicious dishes to choose from. There's also a branch of the restaurant in Manhattan – Ninja New York.

Annalakshmi is a vegetarian restaurant in Chennai, India, with additional restaurants in three other countries. There are no prices on the menu, so guests pay what they can! The people who work there are volunteers and take turns serving customers, cleaning tables, and washing dishes. Indian art covers the walls, and there are even live music and dance performances.

At Dans Le Noir (In the Dark) in Paris, guests order their food in a place with a lot of light, but then they eat in darkness. They focus on the touch, smell, and taste of the food. The waiters there are blind, so when guests are ready to leave, they call their waiter's name. Their waiter then takes them back to the place where they ordered the food. There are additional restaurants in London and Moscow.

**B** Read the webpage again. Write T (true), F (false), or NI (no information) next to the sentences.

1. Guests dress as ninjas at Ninja Akasaka. _____
2. Ninja New York is more popular than Ninja Akasaka. _____
3. Annalakshmi has restaurants in four countries. _____
4. Every guest at Annalakshmi pays the same price. _____
5. Guests never see their food at Dans Le Noir. _____
6. The cooks at Dans Le Noir are blind. _____

**C** Pair work Which restaurants in Part A do you think you'd enjoy? Why? Have you ever been to an unusual restaurant? Tell your partner.

## **2** Listening  So, what did you think?

**A** 🔊 Listen to three couples talk about the restaurants in Exercise 1. Where did each couple eat? Number the restaurants from 1 to 3.

☐ Ninja Akasaka          ☐ Annalakshmi          ☐ Dans Le Noir

**B** 🔊 Listen again. Check (✓) the things each couple liked about the experience.

|      | the service | the prices | the location | the food |
|------|-------------|------------|--------------|----------|
| 1.   | ☐           | ☐          | ☐            | ☐        |
| 2.   | ☐           | ☐          | ☐            | ☐        |
| 3.   | ☐           | ☐          | ☐            | ☐        |

## **3** Writing  A review

**A** Think of a restaurant you like. Answer the questions.

- What is the name of the restaurant?
- What type of food does it serve?
- When were you there last?
- What would you recommend ordering?
- What do you like about the restaurant?

**B** Write a short review of your favorite restaurant. Use the model and your answers from Part A to help you.

> *My Favorite Restaurant*
>
> *Seoul Barbecue is my favorite restaurant. It serves delicious, healthy Korean food. I went there last week and loved it. I ordered beef, and I had some small side dishes. I would recommend doing that. It's fun because you cook your own meat at the table. It's a little expensive, but I really liked the service. I'd recommend this restaurant.*

**C Class activity** Post your reviews around the room. Read your classmates' reviews. Then get more information about the restaurant that interests you the most.

## **4** Speaking  Restaurant recommendations

**Pair work** Recommend a good place to go for each situation. Discuss your ideas.

- take an overseas visitor
- meet a big group of friends
- have a child's birthday party
- have a quiet dinner for two
- get a quick, cheap lunch
- enjoy live music

A: *What's a good place to meet a big group of friends?*
B: *How about . . . ? There's a private room for big groups.*

| **I can** describe restaurant experiences. | ✓ |

# Wrap-up

## 1 Quick pair review

**Lesson A** **Brainstorm!** Make a list of menu items. How many do you know? You have two minutes.

**Lesson B** **Do you remember?** Check (✓) the things you can say to order food. You have one minute.

☐ I'll have some French fries, please.  ☐ Can I have the steak, please?
☐ Try the cheesecake, please.  ☐ Let me check that.
☐ What would you like?  ☐ I'd like some pie, please.

**Lesson C** **Find out!** What interesting food have you and your partner both tried? Take turns. You and your partner have two minutes.

**A:** *I've eaten squid.*
**B:** *I haven't. I've eaten . . .*

**Lesson D** **Guess!** Describe a restaurant in your city, but don't say its name. Can your partner guess which one it is? Take turns. You and your partner have two minutes.

**A:** *This restaurant is on Main Street. It has good seafood, and the food is cheap. The service is fantastic.*
**B:** *Is it Big Fish?*
**A:** *Yes, it is.*

## 2 In the real world

What would you like to order? Go online and find a menu for a restaurant in English. Then write about it.

- What's the name of the restaurant?
- What appetizers, main dish, and side dishes would you like to order?
- What drink would you like to try?
- What dessert would you like to eat?

> *Alphabet Café*
> *I'd like to eat at Alphabet Café. I'd like some garlic bread and the spaghetti. . . .*

# Entertainment

| LESSON **A** | LESSON **B** | LESSON **C** | LESSON **D** |
|---|---|---|---|
| • Types of movies<br>• *So*, *too*, *either*, and *neither* | • Asking for suggestions<br>• Giving a suggestion | • Types of music<br>• Determiners | • Reading: "African Superstars!"<br>• Writing: A popular musician |

## Warm-up

a. ☐

b. ☐

c. ☐

d. ☐

e. ☐

f. ☐

**A** Match the words and the pictures.

_____ an amusement park        _____ a dance performance        _____ a play

_____ a concert        _____ a movie        _____ a soccer game

**B** Which of these types of entertainment do you want to go to? Rank them from 1 (really want to go) to 6 (don't really want to go).

**I'm not a fan of dramas.**

## 1 Vocabulary   Types of movies

**A** 🔊 Match the types of movies and the pictures. Then listen and check your answers.

| | | | |
|---|---|---|---|
| a. an action movie | c. a comedy | e. a horror movie | g. a science-fiction movie |
| b. an animated movie | d. a drama | f. a musical | h. a western |

 1. **g**

 2. **d**

 3.

 4.

 5.

 6.

 7.

 8.

**B Pair work** What are your favorite types of movies? Give an example of the types you like. Tell your partner.

*"I love action movies and dramas. My favorite movies are . . ."*

## 2 Language in context   At the movies

**A** 🔊 Listen to two friends at the movies. What type of movie are they watching?

**B** What about you? Are you ever late for movies? Do you like to sit in the front, middle, or back?

## 3 Grammar 🔊 *So, too, either,* and *neither*

| | |
|---|---|
| I'm a fan of science-fiction movies. | I'm not usually late for movies. |
| **So** am I. / I am, **too**. | **Neither** am I. / I'm not, **either**. |
| Oh, I'm not. I like comedies. | Oh, I am. I'm always late. |
| I like to sit in the front row. | I don't buy popcorn. |
| **So** do I. / I do, **too**. | **Neither** do I. / I don't, **either**. |
| Really? I don't. I prefer the back row. | Oh, I do. And I always get a soda. |

**A** Respond to the sentences in two different ways. Use *so, too, either,* or *neither.*
Compare with a partner.

1. I'm not a fan of dramas.    *Neither am I.*      *I'm not, either.*
2. I love animated movies.    _____      _____
3. I'm not interested in action movies.    _____      _____
4. I'm interested in old westerns.    _____      _____
5. I don't watch horror movies.    _____      _____
6. I don't like science-fiction movies.    _____      _____

**B Pair work** Make the sentences in Part A true for you. Respond with *so, too,
either,* or *neither.*

A: *I'm not a fan of dramas.*
B: *Neither am I.* **OR** *Really? I am. My favorite drama is . . .*

## 4 Speaking Movie talk

**A** Complete the sentences with true information.

I like to eat _____ *candy* _____ at the movies.
(snack)

I really like _____ .
(actor or actress)

I'm not a fan of _____ .
(actor or actress)

I want to see _____ .
(name of movie)

I don't really want to see _____ .
(name of movie)

I often see movies at _____ .
(name of theater)

I usually see movies with _____ .
(name of person)

**B Pair work** Take turns reading your sentences. Respond appropriately.

A: *I like to eat candy at the movies.*
B: *Oh, I don't. I like to eat popcorn.*

**C Group work** What movies are playing right now? Which ones do you want to
see? Can you agree on a movie to see together?

## 5 Keep talking!

Go to page **149** for more practice.

*I can talk about my movie habits and opinions.* ☑

## 1 Interactions | Suggestions

**A** What do you like to do on weekends? Who do you usually spend your weekends with? How do you decide what to do?

**B** 🔊 Listen to the conversation. What do they decide to do on the weekend? Then practice the conversation.

**Douglas:** What do you want to do this weekend?
**Jocelyn:** I don't really know. Do you have any suggestions?
**Douglas:** Well, there's an outdoor movie in the park, a food festival, and a karaoke contest.

**Jocelyn:** I hate karaoke, and we went to the movies last week.
**Douglas:** Let's go to the food festival.
**Jocelyn:** OK. That sounds good. Have you ever been to one?
**Douglas:** No, but it sounds like a lot of fun.

**C** 🔊 Listen to the expressions. Then practice the conversation again with the new expressions.

| Asking for suggestions | Giving a suggestion |
|---|---|
| Do you have any suggestions? | Let's . . . |
| What do you suggest? | Why don't we . . . ? |
| Any suggestions? | We could . . . |

**D** Number the sentences from 1 to 8. Then practice with a partner.

_____ **A:** A play? That's not a bad idea.

_____ **A:** I'm not sure. We could see a movie.

__1__ **A:** Let's do something different tonight.

_____ **A:** Why don't we see the comedy?

_____ **B:** We always see movies. Why don't we see a play?

_____ **B:** OK. And let's have dinner before.

_____ **B:** There are two plays. One is a drama, the other a comedy.

__2__ **B:** OK. What do you suggest?

## 2 Listening Let's get together!

**A** 🔊 Listen to three conversations. Check (✓) what the people decide to do.

| What they decide to do | | Place | Time |
|---|---|---|---|
| 1. ☐ go to a movie | ☐ watch a movie at home | | |
| 2. ☐ go out to eat | ☐ order take-out food | | |
| 3. ☐ go to a play | ☐ go to a baseball game | | |

**B** 🔊 Listen again. Where and when are they going to meet? Write the place and time.

## 3 Speaking This weekend

**A Pair work** Complete the chart with what is happening this weekend where you live.

| | Movies | Music | Sports | Festivals |
|---|---|---|---|---|
| Friday | | | | |
| Saturday | | | | |
| Sunday | | | | |

**B Pair work** Work with a new partner. Look at your charts. Decide to do three things together.

A: *Let's do something fun this weekend.*
B: *All right. Any suggestions?*
A: *Well, we could see the new horror movie. Do you like horror movies?*
B: *No, I don't. Sorry. Why don't we . . . ?*

*I can* ask for and give suggestions. ☑

# C  *All of us love music.*

## 1 Vocabulary  Types of music

**A** ◖))) Listen to the song clips. Number the types of music you hear from 1 to 10. Then check your answers.

pop          rock          jazz          country          classical

folk          hip-hop          techno          reggae          blues

**B** **Pair work**  Say the name of a musician for each type of music in Part A. Tell your partner.

*"Jennifer Lopez sings pop music."*

## 2 Conversation  A music recital

**A** ◖))) Listen and practice.

**Ingrid:** These kids are great musicians. Do all of the students at this school learn a musical instrument?

**John:** No, I don't think so, but most of them do.

**Ingrid:** I see. And do most of the schools in this city have bands?

**John:** I'm not sure. I know a lot of them around here do. Some of the schools even have their own jazz bands.

**Ingrid:** How interesting! So, do you know what's next?

**John:** I think there's going to be a violin solo.

**B** ◖))) Listen to their conversation after the recital. What type of music do the children prefer to play?

# 3 Grammar 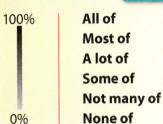 Determiners

| | |
|---|---|
| 100% | **All of** |
| | **Most of** |
| | **A lot of** the students learn a musical instrument. |
| | **Some of** |
| | **Not many of** |
| 0% | **None of** |

**A** Look at the picture of the Branson family. Complete the sentences with determiners. Then compare with a partner.

1. _____ of them are singing.
2. _____ of them have costumes.
3. _____ of them are sitting.
4. _____ of them are playing an instrument.
5. _____ of them have blond hair.
6. _____ of them are dancing.

**B** Make true sentences using determiners. Tell your partner.

1. . . . of my favorite songs are pop songs.
2. . . . of my friends play an instrument.
3. . . . of my classmates play in rock bands.
4. . . . of my friends enjoy singing karaoke.

# 4 Pronunciation Reduction of *of*

**A** Listen and repeat. Notice how *of* is sometimes pronounced /ə/ before consonant sounds.

| /ə/ | /ə/ | /ə/ |
|---|---|---|
| All of the students | A lot of the schools | None of my friends |

**B** **Pair work** Practice the sentences in Exercise 3A. Reduce *of* to /ə/.

# 5 Speaking Ask the class.

**A** **Class activity** Add a type of music, a song, or a singer to the question. Then ask your classmates the question. Write the number of people who answer "yes."

Do you like _____ ? ☐

**B** Share your information. Use determiners.

*"Some of us like hip-hop music."*

# 6 Keep talking!

Go to page 150 for more practice.

I can report the results of a survey. ☑

# D Musicians from around the world

## 1 Reading 🔊

**A** Read the magazine article. Where is each singer from?

### African Superstars!

Algeria's Khaled is extremely popular in France and in the Arab world. He sings *rai*, folk music from his native Algeria that includes French, Spanish, African, and Arabic influences. *Rai* means "opinion" in Arabic, and sometimes people call Khaled "the King of Rai." He recorded his first song at age 14.

Suzanna Owiyo grew up in a family of 14. She is a singer and guitarist from Kenya. She sings in several languages, and her musical styles include local Kenyan pop, folk, and reggae. She uses traditional instruments in all of her songs. Her songs are often about women's and children's rights.

Cesária Évora only became famous internationally at age 47. She doesn't wear shoes on stage because she wants people to remember her native Cape Verde's poor women and children. Cesária sings *morna*, a traditional type of music. She says "*morna* is like the blues" because it talks about the hard lives some people live.

Youssou N'Dour is one of Africa's greatest singers. He mixes traditional music from his native Senegal with hip-hop, jazz, and samba. He gives concerts around the world. His songs are about ending poverty and making the world a healthier and better place. He started a project to open Internet cafés in Africa.

**B** Read the article again. Answer the questions.

1. Where is Khaled's music popular? _____

2. What does Suzanna Owiyo always use in her music? _____

3. Why doesn't Cesária Évora wear shoes on stage? _____

4. What kind of music does Youssou N'Dour play? _____

**C** **Group work** What singers or musicians in your country are internationally famous? What kind of music do they play? What do you think of their music? Discuss your ideas.

## **2** Listening  Classical music hour

**A** 🔊 Listen to a radio host talk about the musician Lang Lang. Where is Lang Lang from?

**B** 🔊 Listen again. Check (✓) the correct answers.

1. Lang Lang had his first music lessons at age:
   ☐ three          ☐ five

2. He received his first award at age:
   ☐ five          ☐ fifteen

3. He likes to share music with:
   ☐ young people      ☐ older people

4. He also works with:
   ☐ UNICEF          ☐ United Nations University

5. Besides classical music, he loves:
   ☐ jazz and rock      ☐ jazz, hip-hop, and pop

## **3** Writing  A popular musician

**A** Think of your favorite musician or a popular musician. Answer the questions.

- Where is this person from?
- What type of music is this musician famous for?
- What is this person's best song?
- What is interesting about this person?

**B** Write a short description about the musician. Use the model and your answers from Part A to help you.

> *My Favorite Singer*
> My favorite singer is Thalia. She's from Mexico.
> She sings different types of music, but mostly
> she sings pop and dance music. My favorite song is
> "No, No, No." She records songs in many languages.
> She sings in English, Spanish, French, and Tagalog.

**C** **Group work**  Share your writing. Did any of you write about the same musician?

## **4** Speaking  Make a playlist

**A** **Pair work**  Make a list of the most important singers, bands, or musicians from your country. What are their most popular songs?

**B** **Pair work**  Create a 5-track playlist. Use your notes.

A: *I think . . . is very important.*
B: *So do I. A lot of young people like his music.*

**C** **Group work**  Present your playlist and explain your choices. Ask and answer questions to get more information.

> *I can* describe important singers and musicians.  ☑

# Wrap-up

## 1 Quick pair review

**Lesson A  Find out!**  What are two types of movies both you and your partner like? You have two minutes.

**A:** *I like action movies. Do you?*
**B:** *No, but I like animated movies. Do you?*

**Lesson B  Do you remember?**  Match the questions with the suggestions. You have one minute.

1. We should see a movie. Do you have any suggestions? _____
2. I'm hungry. Any suggestions? _____
3. Let's get some exercise. What do you suggest? _____
4. Where should we go shopping? Any suggestions? _____
5. We need to take a vacation. What do you suggest? _____

a. We could take a walk.
b. Why don't we go to the market?
c. We could see a comedy.
d. Why don't we go to Mexico?
e. Let's make pizza!

**Lesson C  Brainstorm!**  Make a list of types of music. How many do you know? Take turns. You and your partner have two minutes.

**Lesson D  Guess!**  Describe a popular band or singer, but don't say the name. Can your partner guess the name? Take turns. You and your partner have two minutes.

**A:** *She sings pop music. She sings in Chinese and Korean. She's also an actress.*
**B:** *Jang Nara?*
**A:** *Yes.*

## 2 In the real world

What were some of the top movies this year? Go online and find information about one of them in English. Then write about it.

- What's the name of the movie?
- What actors are in it?
- What type of movie is it?
- What songs are in the movie?

*A Top Movie*
*. . . was one of the top movies this year. It's an animated movie. . . .*

# Time for a change

| LESSON **A** | LESSON **B** | LESSON **C** | LESSON **D** |
|---|---|---|---|
| • Personal goals<br>• Infinitives of purpose | • Reacting to bad news<br>• Reacting to good news | • Milestones<br>• *Will* for predictions; *may, might* for possibility | • Reading: A magazine article<br>• Writing: A dream come true |

## Warm-up

**1**

**2**

**3**

**4**

hola

**5**

**6**

**A** The people in the pictures have made changes in their lives. What change do you think each person made?

**B** Would you like to make any of these changes? Which ones?

# A Personal change

## 1 Vocabulary Personal goals

**A** 🔊 Match the words and the pictures. Then listen and check your answers.

| | | |
|---|---|---|
| a. get a credit card | d. lose weight | g. save money |
| b. join a gym | e. make more friends | h. start a new hobby |
| c. learn an instrument | f. pass a test | i. work / study harder |

1. ☐

2. ☐

3. ☐

4. ☐

5. ☐

6. ☐

7. ☐

8. ☐

9. ☐

**B Pair work** Which things in Part A are easy to do? Which are more difficult? Why? Tell your partner.

*"It's difficult to learn an instrument. It takes a long time!"*

## 2 Language in context I'm making it happen!

**A** 🔊 Listen to three people talk about changes. Who's learning something new?

My friends and I are starting our own band next year. I can sing, but I can't play an instrument, so I'm taking a class to learn the guitar.

*– Leonardo*

I joined a gym last month to lose weight. I only want to lose a couple of kilos, but I'm finding it difficult. But I'm making some new friends, so that's good.

*– Mark*

I hated taking the bus to work, so I saved money to buy a bike. Now I ride it to work every day, and I feel a lot healthier and happier.

*– Tina*

**B** Talk about a change you made.

## 3 Grammar 🔊 Infinitives of purpose

| | |
|---|---|
| I'm taking a class **to learn** the guitar. | (= because I want to learn the guitar) |
| I joined a gym last month **to lose** weight. | (= because I want to lose weight) |
| She'd like to save money **to buy** a bike. | (= because she wants to buy a bike) |
| We're starting a book club in July **to make** more friends. | (= because we want to make more friends) |

**A** Match the sentence parts. Then compare with a partner.

1. I joined a gym last week          to buy a car.
2. I'm saving my money          to get better grades.
3. I'd like to go to the U.S.          to relax.
4. I studied harder          to improve my English.
5. I listen to music          to lose weight.

**B** Rewrite these sentences. Use an infinitive of purpose. Then compare with a partner.

1. I'd like to go to a hair salon because I want to get a new hairstyle.

   *I'd like to go to a hair salon to get a new hairstyle.*

2. I listen to songs in English because I want to improve my listening.

   _____

3. I saved my money because I wanted to buy a new computer.

   _____

4. I'm studying on weekends because I want to get a better job.

   _____

**C Pair work** Which sentences from Part B are true for you? Tell your partner.

## 4 Speaking Three changes

**A** Complete the chart with three changes you would like to make. Then think about the reasons why you would like to make each change.

| | Changes | Reasons |
|---|---|---|
| 1. | | |
| 2. | | |
| 3. | | |

**B Group work** Discuss your changes. Are any of your changes or reasons the same?

*"I'd like to go to Canada to study English. I hope to be an English teacher someday."*

## 5 Keep talking!

Go to page 151 for more practice.

*I can* give reasons for personal changes. ☑

## 1 Interactions     Good and bad news

**A** Do you ever see old classmates or friends around town? What kinds of things do you talk about?

**B** 🔊 Listen to the conversation. What's changed for Emily? Then practice the conversation.

**Joe:** Hey, Emily. Long time no see.
**Emily:** Oh, hi, Joe. How are you doing?
**Joe:** Fine. Well, actually, I didn't pass my driving test – again. That's three times now.
**Emily:** That's too bad.
**Joe:** Yeah, I wanted to drive to the beach this weekend. So, what's new with you?

**Emily:** Well, I'm playing guitar in a band. I'm really enjoying it.
**Joe:** That's wonderful! What kind of music?
**Emily:** Rock. We have a show next week. Do you want to come? I'll email you the information.
**Joe:** Thanks. I'll be there!

**C** 🔊 Listen to the expressions. Then practice the conversation again with the new expressions.

| Reacting to bad news |
| --- |
| That's too bad. |
| That's a shame. |
| I'm sorry to hear that. |

| Reacting to good news |
| --- |
| That's wonderful! |
| That's great to hear! |
| I'm happy to hear that! |

**D** **Pair work**  Share the news below and react appropriately.

I'm learning German.            I lost my wallet.

I bought a car.                 I won two concert tickets.

I failed my math exam.          I'm going to travel to London.

I have a part-time job.         I'm not sleeping well.

I broke my foot.                I'm planning to get a pet.

## 2 Listening  Sharing news

**A** Look at the pictures in Part B. Where are the people?

**B** 🔊 Listen to four people share news with friends. What news are they talking about? Number the pictures from 1 to 4.

**C** 🔊 Listen again. Correct the false sentences. Then compare with a partner.

1. Mark has some free time in the afternoons and evenings.
2. Lucia is saving her money to buy a restaurant.
3. Jeff is taking the train because his new car is not running very well.
4. Wendy and her cousin had a terrible time in Rome and Florence.

## 3 Speaking  Good news, bad news

**A** Complete the chart with some good news and bad news. (Don't use true news!)

| | Good news | | Bad news |
|---|---|---|---|
| 1. | | 1. | |
| 2. | | 2. | |

**B** **Class activity** Share your news. React appropriately.

A: *Hi, Mariko. What's new with you?*
B: *Well, I'm going to Paris next week to study French.*
A: *That's wonderful!*
B: *What's new with you?*

**C** **Group work** Share the most interesting news you heard.

*I can react to good and bad news.* ✓

# C  *I think I'll get a job.*

## 1 Vocabulary  Milestones

**A** 🔊 Complete the chart with the correct milestones. Then listen and check your answers.

- ☐ buy a house
- ☐ get promoted
- ☐ go to college
- ☐ graduate from high school
- ☐ rent an apartment
- ☐ retire
- ☐ start a career
- ☐ get married
- ☐ start school

| Personal milestones | Educational milestones | Work-related milestones |
|---|---|---|
| _____ | _____ | _____ |
| _____ | _____ | _____ |
| _____ | _____ | _____ |

**B** Number the milestones from 1 to 9 in the order they usually happen. Then compare with a partner.

## 2 Conversation  I'll go traveling.

**A** 🔊 Listen and practice.

**Tim:** Hey, Craig. How are you doing?
**Craig:** Oh, hi, Tim. I'm fine. What's new with you?
**Tim:** Well, I'm graduating from college this summer.
**Craig:** That's wonderful! What do you think you'll do in September?
**Tim:** I think I'll go traveling with some friends.
**Craig:** That sounds fun, but it won't be cheap.
**Tim:** Yeah, so I may get a job this summer to pay for the trip.

**B** 🔊 Listen to the rest of the conversation. What's new with Craig?

## 3 Grammar 🔊 *Will* for predictions; *may, might* for possibility

What do you think you**'ll do**?

*Predictions*

I think I**'ll go** traveling with some friends.
I **won't get** a roommate.

Do you think you**'ll get** a roommate?
Yes. I**'ll get** one soon.
No. I **won't get** a roommate this year.

*Possibility*

I don't really know. I **may get** a job.
I'm not really sure. I **might buy** a pet.

**A** Circle the correct words. Then practice with a partner.

1. **A:** Do you think you'll buy a house next year?
   **B:** No. I don't have enough money. But **I'll / I may** rent an apartment. I don't know.
2. **A:** What do you think you'll do on your next birthday?
   **B:** **I'll / I might** have a big party, but I'm not sure.
3. **A:** When do you think you'll retire?
   **B:** **I'll / I may** retire at age 65. Most other people do.
4. **A:** Do you think you'll buy a car this year?
   **B:** No, **I won't / I might**. I don't have enough money for one.
5. **A:** Do you think you'll get married after college?
   **B:** I'm not sure. **I'll / I may** get married someday.

**B** **Pair work** Ask and answer the questions in Part A. Answer with your own information.

## 4 Pronunciation Contraction of *will*

🔊 Listen and repeat. Notice how these pronouns + *will* are contracted into one syllable.

I'll   you'll   he'll   she'll   we'll   they'll

## 5 Speaking My future

**A** Write an idea for each of the things below.

1. an important thing to do: _____
2. an exciting thing to do: _____
3. an expensive thing to buy: _____
4. an interesting person to meet: _____

**B** **Pair work** Ask and answer questions about the things in Part A. Use *will, may,* or *might* and these time expressions.

   **A:** *Do you think you'll start your career this year?*
   **B:** *Yes, I think I will. I have an interview this week.*

| Time expressions | |
|---|---|
| this week | this month |
| this weekend | next month |
| next week | this year |

## 6 Keep talking!

Go to page 152 for more practice.

*I can make predictions about the future.*

# D  Dreams and aspirations

## 1 Reading 🔊

**A** Look at this quote. What do you think it means?

*"A life without dreams is like a garden without flowers."* – Gertraude Beese

**B** Read the article. Check (✓) the best title.

☐ Baseball Team Raises Money in Harlem      ☐ Students Raise Money for Baseball Team
☐ How to Get Baseball Equipment              ☐ Dream Comes True for Harlem Teacher

**Two years ago**, high school students Michael Pinsky and David Connor read an article in a newspaper about a school in Harlem, a neighborhood in New York City. The school had a baseball team, but no money to buy balls, team uniforms, or other equipment.

Michael and David had an idea. They decided to help the team get money for the equipment they needed. So the two boys started a project to raise money for the baseball team. They called the project "Home Runs for Harlem." They placed boxes in stores to collect money for the team and sold bracelets with the words "Home Runs for Harlem" on them. Their plan was to give all the money they collected to the school to support the team.

Michael and David's project was a great success. They raised over $9,000. The team bought the equipment they needed: gloves, baseballs, and bats. The school also used some of the money to pay a baseball coach.

After the school in Harlem received the money, Michael and David spoke to the students at the school, and David explained why this was a dream come true. "It's not just about me," he says. "It's for other people. It's for the community."

"I just hope they have a fun time playing baseball, and if they can have the equipment, then that just helps out," says David. David and Michael now plan to raise money for other baseball teams in Harlem.

For their passionate and inspiring efforts to support school baseball programs, the two teenagers were New Yorkers of the Week on one of New York's news stations.

**C** Read the article again. Number the events from 1 to 8.

_____ They spoke to students in Harlem.          _____ They sold bracelets and collected money.
_____ The school received baseball equipment.     _____ The school hired a coach.
_____ They created "Home Runs for Harlem."        _____ They raised over $9,000.
_____ David and Michael read about a school.      _____ They decided they wanted to help.

**D Group work** Have you or your school ever raised money for something? How did you do it? Do you remember how much you raised? Discuss your experiences.

## 2 Listening An interview with an athlete

**A** 🔊 Listen to an interview with Suzanne, a marathon runner. Check (✓) the two dreams she's achieved.

☐ to run marathons
☐ to go back to school
☐ to win the Chicago Marathon
☐ to run all the big marathons

**B** 🔊 Listen again. Circle the correct answers.

1. This is Suzanne's **fifth** / **seventh** marathon.
2. She **won** / **didn't win** the Boston Marathon.
3. She finished **first** / **last** in her first race in high school.
4. At age **39** / **43**, she decided to make some changes in her life.
5. The most difficult thing for her was the **training** / **stress**.

## 3 Writing A dream come true

**A** Think of a dream that came true for you. Answer the questions.

- What was your dream?
- Why was it a dream for you?
- How did your dream come true?

**B** Write about your dream. Use the model and your answers in Part A to help you.

> *My Dream*
> *My dream was to study Mexican cooking in Oaxaca. I loved to cook, but I wasn't a very good cook. So I went to Oaxaca to study Mexican cooking. I took a two-week class. It was a dream come true. Now I can make great meals. Who knows? I might become a chef someday.*

**C** **Group work** Share your writing. Ask and answer questions for more information.

## 4 Speaking Dream planner

**A** Complete the chart with a dream for the future. Then add three things you'll need to do to achieve it.

| My dream | | How I'll make it happen |
|---|---|---|
| | 1. | |
| | 2. | |
| | 3. | |

**B** **Group work** Tell your group about your dream and how you'll achieve it.

A: *My dream is to start my own business someday.*
B: *That's a great dream. How will you make it happen?*
A: *Well, first I'll go back to school. Then I'll get a job to get some experience.*

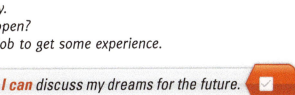

*I can discuss my dreams for the future.* ☑

# Wrap-up

## 1 Quick pair review

**Lesson A** **Brainstorm!** Make a list of personal goals that people can have. How many do you know? You have two minutes.

**Lesson B** **Do you remember?** Write B for ways to react to bad news. Write G for ways to react to good news. You have one minute.

1. _____ That's too bad.
2. _____ I'm sorry to hear that.
3. _____ That's wonderful!
4. _____ I'm happy to hear that!
5. _____ That's a shame.
6. _____ That's great to hear!

**Lesson C** **Find out!** What are two things both you and your partner think you will do in the future? Take turns. You and your partner have two minutes.

A: *I think I'll go to college in two years.*
B: *I don't think I will. I may travel first.*

**Lesson D** **Guess!** Describe a dream you had when you were a child. Can your partner guess what it was? Take turns. You and your partner have two minutes.

A: *I loved swimming. I wanted to win a gold medal.*
B: *Did you want to swim in the Olympics?*
A: *Yes, I did.*

## 2 In the real world

What future goals do famous people have? Do you think they will achieve them? Go online and find information in English about a famous person in one of these categories. Then write about him or her.

| an actor | an athlete | a businessperson | a politician | a scientist | a singer |

*Bill Gates*
*Bill Gates wants to improve people's health. I think he'll achieve this goal. . . .*

# Which product is . . . ?

**A Pair work** Add two more products to the chart. Then think of two examples you know for each product and write their names in the chart.

|  | Example 1 | Example 2 |  |
|---|---|---|---|
| Video game |  |  | Which is newer?<br>Which is more fun?<br>Which is . . . ? |
| Computer |  |  | Which is easier to use?<br>Which is faster?<br>Which is . . . ? |
| Cell phone |  |  | Which is thinner?<br>Which is less expensive?<br>Which is . . . ? |
| Car |  |  | Which is smaller?<br>Which is faster?<br>Which is . . . ? |
|  |  |  |  |
|  |  |  |  |

**B** Compare each pair of products. Use the questions in Part A and your own ideas.

A: *I think . . . is newer than . . . .*
B: *That's right. It's more fun, too.*
A: *I don't really agree. I think . . . is more fun. My friends and I can play it all day!*

**C** Share your comparisons with the class. Which product is better? Why?

# They aren't big enough!

## Student A

**Pair work** You and your partner have pictures of the same people, but there are eight differences. Describe the pictures and ask questions to find the differences. Circle them.

A: *In my picture, Nancy's pants are too baggy. They look very uncomfortable.*
B: *In my picture, Nancy's pants are too tight. So that's different.*
A: *What about Maria's pants? I think they're too short.*
B: *They're too short in my picture, too. So that's the same.*

# From the past

### Student A

**A Pair work** You and your partner have information about six famous people from the past, but some information is missing. Ask these questions and complete the information.

- Where was . . . born?
- When was . . . born?
- What did . . . do?
- Why was . . . famous?

| | | | |
|---|---|---|---|
| **Name** | **George Washington** | **Frida Kahlo** | **Charlie Chaplin** |
| **Place of birth** | the U.S. | Mexico | England |
| **Date of birth** | February 22, 1732 | July 6, 1907 | _____ |
| **What did** | _____ | painter | actor and director |
| **Why famous** | He was the first president of the U.S. | She was very _____ , and her art was _____ . | He was in a lot of funny black-and-white movies. |

| | | | |
|---|---|---|---|
| **Name** | **Jesse Owens** | **Marie Curie** | **Yuri Gagarin** |
| **Place of birth** | the U.S. | _____ | Russia |
| **Date of birth** | September 12, 1913 | November 7, 1867 | March 9, 1934 |
| **What did** | athlete | scientist | astronaut |
| **Why famous** | He was the first American to win _____ gold _____ in track and field in one Olympics. | She was the first person to win two Nobel Prizes. | He was the first person in _____ . |

**B Pair work** Look at the information. What similarities can you find between these people and other famous people you know.

# What can you do here?

**A** **Pair work** Think about where you live. Where can you do each of these things? Take notes.

hear live music

see interesting dance

buy fun souvenirs

eat good, cheap food

see statues and art

enjoy beautiful views

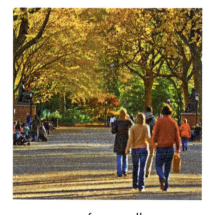
go for a walk

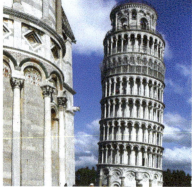
visit historical sites

enjoy nature

**A:** *You can often hear live music at the city square.*
**B:** *Right. And there's also the university coffee shop.*
**A:** *That's true. They have live music on Fridays and Saturdays.*

**B** **Group work** Share your information. How similar are your ideas?

# City quiz

**A** **Pair work** Take the quiz. Ask the questions and guess the answers. Take turns.

1. What is the biggest city in North America?
   **a.** Mexico City          **b.** Los Angeles          **c.** Washington, D.C.

2. Where is the biggest soccer stadium in South America?
   **a.** Buenos Aires, Argentina   **b.** Rio de Janeiro, Brazil   **c.** Lima, Peru

3. "The Big Apple" is the nickname for what U.S. city?
   **a.** Boston          **b.** Washington, D.C.          **c.** New York City

4. Which city is on the Han River?
   **a.** New Orleans, U.S.          **b.** Venice, Italy          **c.** Seoul, South Korea

5. What is the most expensive city?
   **a.** Tokyo, Japan          **b.** London, England          **c.** Rome, Italy

6. What is the safest big city in the U.S.?
   **a.** New York City          **b.** Las Vegas          **c.** Boston

7. The oldest subway system in the world is in what European city?
   **a.** Paris, France          **b.** Madrid, Spain          **c.** London, England

8. Which city has the worst traffic in the U.S.?
   **a.** Chicago          **b.** Los Angeles          **c.** San Francisco

9. What city is in both Europe and Asia?
   **a.** Berlin, Germany          **b.** Stockholm, Sweden          **c.** Istanbul, Turkey

10. The biggest public square in the world is in what city?
    **a.** Beijing, China          **b.** Moscow, Russia          **c.** London, England

**B** Check your answers on the bottom of this page. How many did you get correct?

**C** **Pair work** Think of another question and three possible answer choices. Ask another pair. Do they know the answer?

*"What's the largest city in . . . ?"*

1.a 2.b 3.c 4.c 5.a 6.a 7.c 8.b 9.c 10.a

# They aren't big enough!

### Student B

**Pair work** You and your partner have pictures of the same people, but there are eight differences. Describe the pictures and ask questions to find the differences. Circle them.

**A:** *In my picture, Nancy's pants are too tight. They look very uncomfortable.*
**B:** *In my picture, Nancy's pants are too baggy. So that's different.*
**A:** *What about Maria's pants? I think they're too short.*
**B:** *They're too short in my picture, too. So that's the same.*

# From the past

### Student B

**A** **Pair work** You and your partner have information about six famous people from the past, but some information is missing. Ask these questions and complete the information.

- Where was . . . born?
- What did . . . do?
- When was . . . born?
- Why was . . . famous?

| | | | |
|---|---|---|---|
| **Name** | **George Washington** | **Frida Kahlo** | **Charlie Chaplin** |
| **Place of birth** | the U.S. | _____ | England |
| **Date of birth** | February 22, 1732 | July 6, 1907 | April 16, 1889 |
| **What did** | politician | painter | actor and director |
| **Why famous** | He was the first _____ of the _____ . | She was very creative, and her art was interesting. | He was in a lot of _____ black-and-white _____ . |

| | | | |
|---|---|---|---|
| **Name** | **Jesse Owens** | **Marie Curie** | **Yuri Gagarin** |
| **Place of birth** | the U.S. | Poland | Russia |
| **Date of birth** | _____ | November 7, 1867 | March 9, 1934 |
| **What did** | athlete | scientist | _____ |
| **Why famous** | He was the first American to win four gold medals in track and field in one Olympics. | She was the first person to win _____ Nobel _____ . | He was the first person in space. |

**B** **Pair work** Look at the information. What similarities can you find between these people and other famous people you know.

# What an inspiring person!

**A** Think of three people you admire. Use the categories below or think of your own. Then complete the chart.

| | | | | |
|---|---|---|---|---|
| an athlete | a musician | a writer | an artist | a scientist |
| a politician | an actor / actress | a business leader | a family member | a teacher |

| | Name | Why | Notes |
|---|---|---|---|
| 1. | | | |
| 2. | | | |
| 3. | | | |

**B** **Group work** Share your ideas. Ask and answer questions to get more information.

A: *I really admire Sergey Brin and Larry Page. They started Google.*
B: *Why do you admire them?*
A: *Well, I think they're both talented and intelligent.*
C: *Do you think they're also . . . ?*

**C** Is there a famous person who you *don't* admire? Why not?

# A one-of-a-kind menu

**A** **Group work** Imagine you're going to open a restaurant together. Answer the questions and create a menu.

- What's the name of your restaurant?
- What do you want to serve?
- Is it a cheap or an expensive restaurant? Write the prices.

_____ Restaurant

~ **APPETIZERS** ~

~ **MAIN DISHES** ~

~ **SIDE DISHES** ~

~ **DESSERTS** ~

~ **DRINKS** ~

**A:** *Let's have three or four appetizers.*
**B:** *OK. How about some garlic bread and onion soup?*
**C:** *That sounds good. Let's have a salad, too. How about . . . ?*

**B** **Group work** Exchange your menus. Ask and answer questions about the items. Which dishes would you order?

**A:** *The Mexican salad sounds interesting. What's in it?*
**B:** *It has lettuce, tomatoes, onions, peppers, beans, and corn.*

# Yes, I have!

**Group work** Play the game. Put a small object on *Start*. Toss a coin.

 Move 1 space.     Move 2 spaces.

Heads                                          Tails

Use the words to ask and answer questions. Ask your own *Have you ever . . . ?*
questions on the **Free question** spaces. Take turns.

**A:** *Have you ever made French fries?*
**B:** *Yes, I have.*

# Movie favorites

**A** Complete the chart with six types of movies that you like. Add a title for each type.

|   | Type of movie | Title of movie |
|---|---|---|
| 1. | | |
| 2. | | |
| 3. | | |
| 4. | | |
| 5. | | |
| 6. | | |

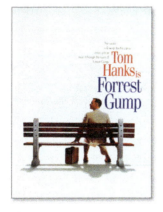

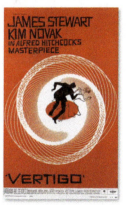

**B** **Class activity**  Find classmates who like the same types of movies you like.
Then ask questions with *Have you ever . . . ?*

A: *I really like animated movies.*
B: *So do I.*
A: *Really? Have you ever seen Spirited Away?*
B: *Yes, I have. I love that movie!*

# Class survey

**A** Complete the questions with your own ideas.

1. Do you like the band _____ ?
   (a band)  ☐

2. Do you like the song _____ ?
   (a song title)  ☐

3. Do you have the album _____ ?
   (name of an album)  ☐

4. Do you ever listen to _____ ?
   (a type of music)  ☐

5. Do you know the words to the song _____ ?
   (name of a song)  ☐

6. Did you listen to _____ as a child?
   (a type of music)  ☐

7. Would you like to see _____ in concert?
   (a singer or band)  ☐

**B** **Class activity** Ask your classmates the questions in Part A. How many people said "yes" to each question? Write the total number in the boxes.

**C** **Pair work** Share your information.

    **A:** *A lot of our classmates like the band . . .*
    **B:** *That's interesting. Not many of us like the band . . .*

**D** Share the most interesting information with the class.

*"All of us would like to see . . . in concert."*

# Why did I do that?

**A** Think about things that you did in the past. Check (✓) the things in the first column that are true for you. Then add three more things.

☐ I took a long trip                          to _____ .

☐ I sent a text to someone              to _____ .

☐ I took a test                                  to _____ .

☐ I joined a gym                              to _____ .

☐ I got a cell phone                        to _____ .

☐ I uploaded some photos              to _____ .

☐ I worked hard                              to _____ .

☐ I got a part-time job                    to _____ .

☐ _____                        to _____ .

☐ _____                        to _____ .

☐ _____                        to _____ .

**B** Why did you do each thing? Complete the sentences in Part A with an infinitive of purpose. Use the ideas below or think of your own.

| talk with my friends | learn an instrument | show my friends |
|---|---|---|
| get my driver's license | get some experience | get a job |
| share good news | buy a gift | make more friends |
| save money | lose weight | see my relatives |

**C** **Group work** Share your sentences. Ask and answer questions for more information.

A: *I took a long trip to see my relatives.*
B: *When was that?*
A: *Last year.*
C: *Where did you go?*
A: *I went . . .*

# Next year . . .

**A** Add two future activities to the chart.

| Do you think you'll . . . next year? | Name | Other details |
|---|---|---|
| take a trip with your family | | |
| start a new hobby | | |
| join a gym | | |
| get married | | |
| buy something expensive | | |
| move to a different home | | |
| start a career | | |
| learn a musical instrument | | |
| | | |
| | | |

**B** **Class activity** Find classmates who will do each thing. Write their names. Ask and answer questions for more information. Take notes.

**A:** *Jun, do you think you'll take a trip with your family next year?*
**B:** *Yes, I do.*
**A:** *Really? Where will you go?*
**B:** *We're planning to go to Australia to see some friends. I hope to . . .*

  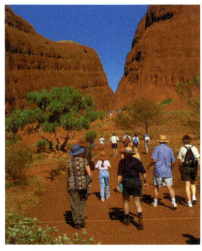

**C** **Group work** Share the most interesting information.

# Irregular verbs

| Base form | Simple past | Past participle |
|-----------|-------------|-----------------|
| be | was, were | been |
| become | became | become |
| build | built | built |
| buy | bought | bought |
| choose | chose | chosen |
| come | came | come |
| do | did | done |
| draw | drew | drawn |
| drink | drank | drunk |
| drive | drove | driven |
| eat | ate | eaten |
| feel | felt | felt |
| get | got | gotten |
| give | gave | given |
| go | went | gone |
| hang | hung | hung |
| have | had | had |
| hear | heard | heard |
| hold | held | held |
| know | knew | known |
| leave | left | left |
| lose | lost | lost |
| make | made | made |

| Base form | Simple past | Past participle |
|-----------|-------------|-----------------|
| meet | met | met |
| pay | paid | paid |
| put | put | put |
| read | read | read |
| ride | rode | ridden |
| run | ran | run |
| say | said | said |
| see | saw | seen |
| sell | sold | sold |
| send | sent | sent |
| sing | sang | sung |
| sit | sat | sat |
| sleep | slept | slept |
| speak | spoke | spoken |
| spend | spent | spent |
| stand | stood | stood |
| swim | swam | swum |
| take | took | taken |
| teach | taught | taught |
| think | thought | thought |
| wear | wore | worn |
| win | won | won |
| write | wrote | written |

# Credits

## Illustration credits

Tom Garrett: 65, 69, 115; John Goodwin: 103; Kim Johnson: 70, 71, 80, 100, 110, 119; Bill Ledger: 86, 106, 121; Dean MacAdam: 90, 107, 111, 117, 120, 140, 144; Garry Parsons: 66, 97, 139; Cristina Sampaio: 116; Rob Schuster: 66, 69, 89, 148

## Text credits

The authors and publishers are grateful for permission to reprint the following items: 122 Adapted from "NYers Of The Week: Two Students Raise Funds For Harlem Baseball Teams" by Josh Robin, www.ny1.com, June 19, 2009. Copyright © 2010. Reprinted with permission from NY1 News. Every effort has been made to trace the owners of copyrighted material in this book. We would be grateful to hear from anyone who recognizes his or her copyrighted material and who is unacknowledged. We will be pleased to make the necessary corrections in future editions of the book.

## Photography credits

67 (all) ©Shutterstock; 68 (both) ©Frank Veronsky; 70 (clockwise from top left) ©Shutterstock; ©Photo Edit; ©Caro/Alamy; ©Media Bakery; ©Shutterstock; ©Inmagine; ©Robin Lynne Gibson/Getty Images; ©Jean-Michel Volat/Getty Images; 72 (left to right) ©John Lander/Alamy; ©Alamy; ©Chen Chao/Getty Images; 73 (top to bottom) ©Arco Images/Alamy; ©Craig Lovell/Alamy; 75 (clockwise from top left) ©Shutterstock; ©Getty Images; ©Shutterstock; ©Lou Linwei/Alamy; ©Adrian Buck/Alamy; ©Ian Dagnall/Alamy; 76 (top row, left to right) ©Terry Smith Images/Alamy; ©Media Bakery; ©Glow Images/Getty Images; (middle row, left to right) ©Media Bakery; ©Dirk von Mallinckrodt/Getty Images; ©Media Bakery; ©Michael Snell/Alamy; (bottom row, left to right) ©Alamy; ©Tibor Bognar/Alamy; ©Scott Olson/Getty Images; 77 (left to right) ©Alamy; ©Wendy Connett/Alamy; ©Shutterstock; 78 (left to right) ©Frank Veronsky; ©Balthasar Thomass/Alamy; 79 (top) ©Shutterstock; (middle row, left to right) ©Roger Cracknell/Alamy; ©Nic Cleave Photography/Alamy; ©Shutterstock (bottom row, left to right) ©Alamy; ©Media Bakery; ©Shutterstock; 80 (clockwise from top left) ©Shutterstock; ©Media Bakery; ©Shutterstock; ©Sami Sarkis Provence/Alamy; ©Jeff Spielman/Getty Images; 81 ©Shutterstock; 83 ©Tony Anderson/Getty Images; 85 (left, top to bottom) ©Shutterstock; ©AP/Wide World Photos; ©Alberto E. Rodriguez/Getty Images; ©Ferdaus Shamim/Getty Images; ©Bloomberg/Getty Images; ©Getty Images; (right, top to bottom) ©Eileen Langsley Olympic Images/Alamy; ©Newscom; ©Media Bakery; ©AP/Wide World Photos; ©Shutterstock; ©Getty Images; 86 (left to right) ©Shutterstock; ©NASA/Getty Images; ©AP/Wide World Photos; ©Getty Images; 87 (top to bottom) ©Time & Life Pictures/Getty Images; ©Shutterstock; 88 (both) ©Frank Veronsky; 90 (left to right) ©Shutterstock; ©Pictorial Press Ltd./Alamy; ©Newscom; ©AP/Wide World Photos; 91 ©Jonathan Ferrey/Getty Images; 92 ©AP/Wide World Photos; 93 ©Thomas Coex/Getty Images; 95 (clockwise from top left) ©Paul Collis/Alamy; ©Craig Lovell/Alamy; ©Lonely Planet Images; ©Newscom; ©Nick Hanna/Alamy; ©Dan Galic/Alamy; 96 (top row, left to right) ©Shutterstock; ©Shutterstock; ©Shutterstock; ©Bon Appetit/Alamy; (second row, left to right) ©Bon Appetit/Alamy; ©Inmagine; ©Shutterstock; ©Cristina Cassinelli/Getty Images; (third row, left to right) ©James Baigrie/Getty Images; ©Martin Lee/Alamy; ©Media Bakery; (bottom row, left to right) ©Carlos Davila/Alamy; ©Food Folio/Alamy; ©Shutterstock; ©Shutterstock; 98 (top row, both) ©Frank Veronsky; (bottom row, left to right) ©Jupiter Images/Getty Images; ©Shutterstock; 100 (top row, left to right) ©Shutterstock; ©Inmagine; ©Rusty Hill/Getty Images; ©Inmagine; (bottom row, left to right) ©Alamy; ©Shutterstock; ©Masashi Hayasaka/Getty Images; ©Comstock Images/Getty Images; ©Shutterstock; 101 ©Shutterstock;

102 (top to bottom) ©Ninja Akasaka; ©India Today Group/Getty Images; ©Jack Carey/Alamy; 105 (clockwise from top left) ©Shutterstock; ©Paul Doyle/Alamy; ©Jaime Lopez/Getty Images; ©Insadco Photography/Alamy; ©Media Bakery; ©Jim Havey/Alamy; 106 (clockwise from top left) ©Pixar/Newscom; ©TM/ Dreamworks/Newscom; ©Sony Pictures Entertainment/Everett Collection; ©Everett Collection; ©Mary Evans/Moving Pictures/Ronald Grant/Everett Collection; ©United Film/Everett Collection; ©Universal Pictures/Everett Collection; ©New Line/Everett Collection; 108 (main photo) ©Media Bakery; (insets, top to bottom) ©Joseph De Sciose/Getty Images; ©Richard Levine/Alamy; ©Media Bakery; 109 (clockwise from top left) ©Upper Cut Images/Getty Images; ©Blaine Harrington III/Alamy; ©Shutterstock; ©Shutterstock; 110 (clockwise from top left) ©Shutterstock; ©Fotosearch; ©Bruce Ayres/Getty Images; ©Daniel Dempster Photography/Alamy; ©Media Bakery; ©Blend Images/Getty Images; ©Mark Bassett/Alamy; ©Benjamin Shearn/Getty Images; ©Inmagine; ©Inmagine; 112 (clockwise from top left) ©AFP/Getty Images; ©Getty Images; ©Newscom; ©AFP/Getty Images; 113 (top to bottom) ©AP/ Wide World Photos; 116 (left to right) ©John Parra/Getty Images; ©Media Bakery; ©Shutterstock; ©Yellow Dog Productions/Alamy; 118 (both) ©Frank Veronsky; 120 (top row, left to right) ©Media Bakery; ©Blend Images/Getty Images; ©Design Pics/Ron Nickel/Getty Images; (middle row, left to right) ©Dirk Anschutz/Getty Images; ©Insadco Photography/Alamy; ©Bellurget Jean Louis/ Getty Images; (bottom row, left to right) ©Image Source/Getty Images; ©Blend Images/Getty Images; Age Fotostock; 122 ©Home Runs for Harlem; 123 ©Courtesy of Suzanne Lefebre; 141 (clockwise from top left) ©SuperStock/Getty Images; ©Hulton Archive/Getty Images; Everett Collection; ©Popperfoto/Getty Images; ©Hulton Archive/Getty Images; ©Mary Evans Picture Library/Everett Collection; 142 (clockwise from top left) ©Lonely Planet Images; ©David Lyons/ Alamy; ©Wendy Connett/Getty Images; ©Elan Fleisher/Alamy; ©David R. Frazier/ Alamy; ©Robert Harding Picture Library Ltd./Alamy; 145 (clockwise from top left) ©SuperStock/Getty Images; ©Hulton Archive/Getty Images; Everett Collection; ©Popperfoto/Getty Images; ©Hulton Archive/Getty Images; ©Mary Evans/Everett Collection; 146 (clockwise from top left) ©Newscom; ©Juergen Hasenkopf/Alamy; ©AP/Wide World Photos; ©AP/Wide World Photos; ©AP/Wide World Photos; ©AP/Wide World Photos; ©David R. Anchuelo/Getty Images; 149 (clockwise from top left) ©Kobal; ©Everett Collection; ©Mary Evans/LUCAS FILM/Ronald Grant/Everett Collection; ©Advertising Archive/Everett Collection; ©Pictorial Press Ltd./Alamy; ©Everett Collection; ©Newscom; ©Kobal; 150 ©Newscom; 151 ©Colin Raw/Getty Images; 152 (left to right) ©Alamy; ©David Wall/Alamy; ©Hideo Kurihara/Alamy

# Four Corners

## Jack C. Richards · David Bohlke

**2B**

## Video Activity Sheets

# 7 A farmers' market

## Before you watch

**A** Look at the picture. Circle the correct answers. Then compare with a partner.

1. What is this a picture of?

   a. a supermarket      b. a farmers' market      c. a bake sale

2. What kind of food is *not* in the picture?

   a. fast food      b. fresh food      c. fruits and vegetables

3. Who usually sells the food there?

   a. waiters      b. cooks      c. vendors

**B Pair work**  How many food items can you identify in the picture?

## While you watch

**A** What does Ben buy at the farmers' market? Check (✓) the correct answers.

☐ apple cider  ☐ bread    ☐ eggs     ☐ pasta
☐ apple juice  ☐ carrots  ☐ flowers  ☐ a plant
☐ apples       ☐ cheese   ☐ jam      ☐ potatoes
☐ bananas      ☐ donuts   ☐ milk     ☐ tomatoes

**B** Write T (true) or F (false).

1. The carrots at the supermarket are usually three dollars. _____

2. Ben sometimes bargains for a lower price at the farmers' market. _____

3. Apple cider is like apple jam. _____

4. The bread at the farmers' market is very fresh. _____

5. Nick usually goes grocery shopping at the supermarket. _____

**C** Circle the correct answers.

1. The food at the farmers' market is _____ than the food at the supermarket.

   a. too fresh      b. not fresh enough      c. fresher

2. The food in the supermarket is _____ than the food at the farmers' market.

   a. more expensive      b. less expensive      c. too expensive

3. The farmers' market has great apples in the _____.

   a. summer      b. fall      c. spring

4. Ben's favorite jam is _____.

   a. blueberry      b. strawberry      c. apple

5. Ben says jam and bread are great for _____.

   a. breakfast      b. lunch      c. a snack

6. Ben bought a plant for his _____.

   a. kitchen      b. bedroom      c. living room

## After you watch

**Group work** Discuss the questions.

• What things would you buy at Ben's farmers' market? Why?

• Is there a farmers' market where you live? Do you ever go there?

• Where do you usually buy your food? Why?

• What's better to buy at a farmers' market than at a supermarket? Why?

• What's better to buy at a supermarket than at a farmers' market? Why?

• Do you bargain for a lower price when you shop for food? Why?

# Things to do in New York City for less than $5.00

## Before you watch

**A** Match the words and the places. Then compare with a partner.

| a. bridge | b. ferry | c. library | d. museum | e. statue |

1. ☐

2. ☐

3. ☐

4. ☐

5. ☐

**B** Circle the correct answers. Then compare with a partner.

1. A ferry is a kind of _____.

   a. train     b. bus     c. boat

2. A food cart is a small shop _____ where you can buy food.

   a. on the street     b. in a restaurant     c. at home

3. If something is free, it costs _____.

   a. five dollars     b. less than five dollars     c. nothing

## While you watch

**A** What cheap activities in New York City does Soon-mi recommend? Check (✓) the correct answers.

☐ eat from a food cart    ☐ go to a mall    ☐ go to a zoo    ☐ see a famous statue

☐ go to a dance club    ☐ go to a museum    ☐ ride a ferry boat    ☐ take a train

☐ go to a library    ☐ go to a park    ☐ see a Broadway play    ☐ walk across a bridge

**B** Match Soon-mi's comments and the places they describe.

1. You can see it for free on the ferry. _____
2. I really love the lion statues. _____
3. I think it's about 150 years old. _____
4. Here's one thing you shouldn't miss. _____
5. Everyone thinks it costs twenty dollars. _____

a. New York Public Library
b. Metropolitan Museum of Art
c. Staten Island Ferry
d. Brooklyn Bridge
e. Statue of Liberty

**C** Write T (true) or F (false).

1. Soon-mi lives in New York City. _____
2. The Staten Island Ferry goes between Staten Island and Manhattan. _____
3. The Brooklyn Bridge connects Brooklyn and Staten Island. _____
4. Food carts have a lot of expensive food. _____
5. Canal Street is the busiest street in Chinatown. _____
6. You can use the Internet for free in the Metropolitan Museum. _____
7. The recommended cost to enter the museum is one dollar. _____

## After you watch

**A** **Pair work** Would you like to do any of the activities Soon-mi describes in New York City? What other things would you like to do there? Tell your partner.

*"I'd like to ride the Staten Island Ferry and walk across the Brooklyn Bridge. I'd like to see a Broadway play, too."*

**B** **Group work** What fun activities are free or cheap to do in your town or city? Tell your group.

# unit 9  *An inspiring person*

## Before you watch

**A** Match the verbs and the definitions. Then compare with a partner.

1. admire _____     a. to learn about something

2. inspire _____     b. to give someone knowledge or information

3. study _____     c. to like someone for what he or she does

4. teach _____     d. to make someone want to do something

**B** Complete the sentences with the correct words. Then compare with a partner.

| beautiful    exciting    modern    passionate |
| --- |

1. I am _____ about music. I listen to it every day.

2. Soccer is my favorite sport. I think it's so _____ to watch!

3. This computer uses new technology. It is very _____.

4. I went to Grenada two years ago. The weather was _____ there!

## While you watch

Aunt Gloria

Alicia

**A** In what ways did Aunt Gloria inspire Alicia? Check (✓) the correct answers.
(More than one answer is possible.)

☐ Gloria gave Alicia drawing lessons.          ☐ She taught Alicia about art.

☐ She taught Alicia how to paint.          ☐ She is a famous artist.

☐ She took Alicia to art museums.          ☐ She is passionate about art.

**B** Circle the correct answers.

1. In the video, Alicia _____.

   a. calls her aunt     b. goes to a museum with her aunt     c. visits her aunt

2. Alicia wants to _____.

   a. thank her aunt     b. give her aunt a gift     c. both a and b

3. Alicia's family is from _____.

   a. a very small town     b. a big city     c. a small city

4. The museums in the city had many _____ paintings.

   a. simple and boring     b. old and modern     c. big and small

5. Alicia gives Aunt Gloria _____.

   a. some jewelry     b. a painting     c. an art book

**C** Write T (true) or F (false).

1. Alicia is a high school student. _____

2. She can make her own jewelry. _____

3. She wants to be an actress. _____

4. Aunt Gloria and Alicia went to museums about once a year. _____

5. They want to go to a museum again soon. _____

## After you watch

**A Pair work** Interview your partner. Take notes.

| Questions | Name: _____ |
|---|---|
| 1. Do you know anyone like Aunt Gloria? Who? How are they similar? | |
| 2. Like Alicia, do you have any of the same talents or interests as a family member? Who? | |
| 3. Who inspires you? | |
| 4. How does he or she inspire you? | |
| 5. What personality adjectives describe him or her? | |
| 6. What is he or she passionate about? | |

**B Pair work** Tell another classmate about your partner's answers. Do your partners have similar stories about the people who inspired them?

# 10 *Olga's Diner*

## Before you watch

**A** Label the pictures with the correct words. Then compare with a partner.

> blueberries    a hamburger    soda    strawberries

1. _____  2. _____  3. _____  4. _____

**B** Circle the correct answers. Then compare with a partner.

1. What is a diner?

   a. a type of restaurant    b. a meal    c. a waiter

2. What is a fresh fruit plate?

   a. a plate with fruit painted on it    b. a fruit salad    c. a bag of apples

3. What is dessert?

   a. breakfast    b. sweet food you eat after a meal    c. a side dish

## While you watch

**A** Which food items do Ben and Marco say are on the menu? Check (✓) the correct answers.

☐ carrot juice   ☐ hamburgers   ☐ oysters   ☐ spring rolls
☐ cheesecake   ☐ lamb chops   ☐ rice   ☐ squid
☐ crab cakes   ☐ mixed vegetables   ☐ seaweed salad   ☐ steak
☐ fruit salad   ☐ onion rings   ☐ soy milk   ☐ tomato soup

**B** Who orders what? Draw a line from each food item to Marco or Ben.

Marco

fresh fruit plate

a hamburger

onion rings

mixed vegetables

carrot juice

a large soda

frozen yogurt

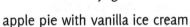

apple pie with vanilla ice cream

Ben

**C** Write T (true) or F (false).

1. The menu at Olga's Diner is really big. _____
2. The service is very fast. _____
3. Olga's Diner is very expensive. _____
4. After dinner, Ben has a stomachache. _____
5. Marco and Ben take a taxi home. _____

Olga's Diner

## After you watch

**A Pair work** Ask and answer the questions.

1. What would you order at Olga's Diner?
2. What wouldn't you try at Olga's Diner?
3. What's the name of a restaurant you haven't been to but want to try? Why?
4. Have you ever had a stomachache after eating in a restaurant? What happened?
5. What restaurant would you recommend in your city or town? Why?

**B** Imagine you have a restaurant. Make a menu of the foods you would serve.

_____

**Appetizers**
_____.....$_____
_____.....$_____
_____.....$_____

**Side Dishes**
_____.....$_____
_____.....$_____
_____.....$_____

**Main Dishes**
_____.....$_____
_____.....$_____
_____.....$_____

**Desserts**
_____.....$_____
_____.....$_____
_____.....$_____

**C Group work** Tell your classmates about the foods on your menu.

*"My restaurant's name is Sofia's Diner. I'd serve . . ."*

# 11 *World music*

## Before you watch

**A** Look at the pictures. Number the pictures from 1 to 3. Then compare with a partner.

1. Someone is interviewing someone else.

2. Someone is telling a story to someone else.

3. Someone is translating a word for someone else.

**B Pair work** When is the last time you did each thing in Part A? Who were you with? Tell your partner.

## While you watch

**A** What types of music do they say they listen to? Check (✓) the correct answers. (More than one answer is possible.)

|  | Emi | Peter | Alicia | Rebecca |
|---|---|---|---|---|
| 1. classical music | ☐ | ☐ | ☐ | ☐ |
| 2. country music | ☐ | ☐ | ☐ | ☐ |
| 3. jazz | ☐ | ☐ | ☐ | ☐ |
| 4. music from movies | ☐ | ☐ | ☐ | ☐ |
| 5. pop music | ☐ | ☐ | ☐ | ☐ |
| 6. pop music from India | ☐ | ☐ | ☐ | ☐ |
| 7. reggae | ☐ | ☐ | ☐ | ☐ |

**B** Write T (true) or F (false).

1. Emi thinks reggae music is relaxing. _____

2. Bob Marley is a famous singer from Nigeria. _____

3. Peter says most of the people in Texas listen to reggae. _____

4. Alicia thinks most Indian pop songs are about pop culture. _____

5. Emi and Rebecca are friends. _____

**C** Circle the correct answers.

1. Peter loves country music because the words are really _____.

    a. inspiring     b. intelligent     c. interesting

2. Peter says a lot of country music songs _____.

    a. are serious     b. tell a story     c. are on the radio

3. Alicia thinks that Indian musical movies are _____.

    a. fun     b. boring     c. interesting

4. Some of Alicia's friends can _____ the words.

    a. sing     b. spell     c. translate

5. Emi and Rebecca plan to go to a _____ concert together.

    a. jazz     b. reggae     c. rock

## After you watch

**A Pair work** Do you listen to any of the same music as Emi, Peter, Alicia, or Rebecca? Why or why not? Tell your partner.

*"I listen to reggae like Emi and Rebecca, because it's relaxing. But I don't listen to classical music like Emi. It's too relaxing. It makes me fall asleep!"*

**B** Make a playlist of songs. Choose songs from all of the types of music that you like.

| Name of song | Singer, musician, group | Type of music |
|---|---|---|
| "One Love" | Bob Marley | Reggae |
| | | |
| | | |
| | | |
| | | |

**C Pair work**  Tell your partner about your playlist. Ask and answer questions for more information.

    A: I love the song "One Love" by Bob Marley.

    B: Why do you love it?

    A: It's a really cool, relaxing reggae song.

# 12 *My dream: Starting a business*

## Before you watch

**A** Label the pictures with the correct words. Then compare with a partner.

| coffee | cookies | a cupcake | a muffin | a recipe |
|--------|---------|-----------|----------|----------|

1. _____   2. _____   3. _____   4. _____   5. _____

**B** Check (✓) the correct answers. Then compare with a partner.

1. What is a business?

☐ It's a job you get after you graduate.

☐ It's a company or organization that sells something to make money.

2. Who are customers?

☐ They're people who buy things.

☐ They're people who sell things.

3. What does it mean to do research?

☐ It means you look for information about something and study it.

☐ It means you prepare for an exam.

## While you watch

**A** Write T (true) or F (false).

1. Tim's dream is to have a cookie store. _____

2. Tim's friends don't think he should open a cookie store. _____

3. Tim talks to Amelia because she has her own shop. _____

4. Amelia says it's really important to know your cupcakes. _____

5. Amelia didn't have any problems making her dream come true. _____

Tim and Amelia

**B** Circle the correct answers.

1. Tim's video is for his business _____.

   a. class     b. bank     c. plan

2. Tim asks Amelia for _____.

   a. her cupcake recipe     b. business advice     c. a job

3. At first, Amelia sold only _____.

   a. coffee and muffins     b. coffee and donuts     c. coffee and cupcakes

4. Amelia thinks Tim might have a problem selling only _____.

   a. coffee     b. cookies     c. cupcakes

5. A business plan shows that a new business will _____.

   a. sell cookies     b. buy new products     c. make money

6. Amelia offers Tim _____.

   a. a business plan     b. a job     c. a cup of coffee

**C** How did Amelia's dream come true? Number the steps from 1 to 7.

_____ She went to the bank for a loan, but the bank said "no."

_____ She used her research to write a business plan.

___1___ She worked part-time at a coffee shop to learn about the business.

_____ The bank liked Amelia's business plan, and it gave her the money.

_____ She went to a second bank, and that bank said "no," too.

_____ She did a lot of research.

_____ She took a class to learn about business.

## After you watch

**A Pair work**  How will Tim make his dream happen? Make predictions. Use the expressions below and your own ideas.

| | | | |
|---|---|---|---|
| do research | get a job | learn about his customers | take another class |
| finish his video report | get a loan | save money | write a business plan |

A: I think Tim will write a business plan.

B: I think he might get a loan.

**B Group work**  Share your predictions with another pair. How many different predictions did you make?

# Credits

**Photography credits**

T-190, T-193, T-194, T-195 *(bottom)*, T-196 *(top)*, T-197, T-199 *(bottom)*
Video screen grabs courtesy of Steadman Productions, Boston, MA

# Four Corners

## Jack C. Richards · David Bohlke

### with Kathryn O'Dell

**2B**

# Workbook

# Contents

# Shopping

## A It's lighter and thinner.

**1** Match the opposites.

1. light ___*e*___      a. loud
2. quiet ___*a*___      b. big
3. cheap ___*f*___      c. fast
4. small ___*b*___      d. thick
5. thin ___*d*___       e. heavy
6. slow ___*c*___       f. expensive

**2** Look at the pictures. Complete the sentences with some of the words from Exercise 1.

1. Joe's car is _____*big*_____ and _____*slow*_____ .

2. Donna's car is _____*small*_____ and _____*fast*_____ .

3. This book is _____*thick*_____ and _____*expensive*_____ .

4. This book is _____*thin*_____ and _____*cheap*_____ .

**3** Look at the pictures. Then write sentences with the comparative form of the adjectives in parentheses.

desktop computer                 laptop

1. *The desktop computer is heavier than the laptop.*   (heavy) ier
2. The desktop computer is bigger than the laptop   (big)
3. The desktop computer is older than the laptop   (old)
4. The desktop computer is lighter than the laptop   (light)
5. The desktop computer is newer than the laptop   (new)
6. The desktop computer is smaller than the laptop   (small)

**4** Circle the correct words to complete the email.

| To: | MateoG@cup.org |
|---|---|
| From: | Cassandra92@cup.com |
| Subject: | My new computer! |

Hi, Mateo!

I have a new computer. It's really nice. It's a laptop, so it's **more small / (smaller)**
1
than my old desktop computer. It's also **(faster) / less fast**! It was
2
**expensiver / more expensive**, but that's OK. I love it! The computer store had
3
a **(cheaper) / less cheap** laptop, but it was very **old / (older)**. My laptop is
4                                                   5
**(better) / good** than that one!
6

Oh, I have a new cell phone, too. It's **nice / (nicer)** than my old phone. It's pretty
7
**small / less small**, and it's extremely **(lighter) / light**!
8                                        9

How are you? How are your Spanish classes? Are they **(more difficult) / difficult**
10
than your classes last year? My English class is **bad / (worse)** than my class last
11
year. The teacher is pretty friendly, but the class is **big / (bigger)** than the one
12
last year!

Write soon!
Cassandra

**5** Complete the conversation with the comparative form of the correct adjective from the box. Use *Which, is, printer*, and *than* as needed.

| cheap | new | quiet | small |
|-------|-----|-------|-------|

**Clerk:** Hello. Can I help you?

**Yoko:** Yes, please. I want to buy a new printer.

**Clerk:** OK. These two printers are great – the Target 1000 and the Excite XL.

**Yoko:** _Which printer is smaller_ ?
    1

**Clerk:** The Target 1000 _____ the
                                              2
Excite XL. The Excite XL is very big.

**Yoko:** _____ ?
                        3

**Clerk:** The Target 1000 _____
                                              4
the Excite XL. It's only $120.

**Yoko:** _____ ?
                        5

**Clerk:** Oh, the Excite XL _____ the Target 1000.
                                              6
The Target 1000 is pretty loud.

**Yoko:** Hmm . . . _____ ?
                                    7

**Clerk:** The Excite XL _____ . The Target 1000 is a year old.
                                              8

**Yoko:** OK, thanks. I want to buy the Excite XL.

**6** Write sentences about the pictures. Use the comparative form of the adjectives.

1. _The bicycle is smaller than the motorcycle._ (small)

2. The bicyde is ~~expen~~ (expensive)

3. _____ (heavy)

4. _____ (quiet)

5. _____ (fast)

bicycle, $1,500

motorcycle, $4,000

**7** What's your opinion? Write sentences about the pictures in Exercise 6. Use the comparative form of the adjectives.

1. _____ (nice)

2. _____ (good)

# B  *Would you take $10?*

**1** Write B (bargaining for a lower price) or S (suggesting a different price). Then add the correct punctuation.

1. __B__   Will you take $100 __?__

2. _____   I'll let you have it for $85 _____

3. _____   You can have it for $15 _____

4. _____   How about $35 _____

5. _____   Would you take $12 _____

6. _____   I'll give it to you for $45 _____

**2** Complete the conversation with some of the sentences from Exercise 1.

**A.**  **Bin:** Excuse me? How much is this plate?

  **Hai:** It's only $20.

  **Bin:** Oh, that's expensive.

  ___Would you take $12___ ?
  <sub>1</sub>

  **Hai:** No, I'm sorry. _____ .
  <sub>2</sub>

  **Bin:** OK, thanks. I'll take it.

**B. Gustavo:** Excuse me? How much is this hat?

  **Ivan:** It's only $60.

  **Gustavo:** Wow, that's expensive.

  _____ ?
  <sub>1</sub>

  **Ivan:** No, I'm sorry. $60 is a good price.

  **Gustavo:** Well, thanks, anyway.

  **Ivan:** Wait! _____ .
  <sub>2</sub>

  **Gustavo:** Great. I'll take it!

# C This hat is too small.

## 1 Circle the correct word to complete each sentence.

1. These jeans are tight. They're not _____ .

   a. bright     b. uncomfortable     c. comfortable

2. This gray shirt is very _____ . Can I try on that shirt with flowers on it?

   a. plain     b. comfortable     c. bright

3. I don't like this dress. It's _____ .

   a. pretty     b. comfortable     c. ugly

4. This blouse is too small. It's very _____ .

   a. baggy     b. tight     c. comfortable

5. I really like this tie. It's so _____ .

   a. uncomfortable     b. nice     c. ugly

6. $200! These shoes are _____ .

   a. expensive     b. baggy     c. bright

## 2 Complete the conversations with the correct adjective from the box.

| bright | comfortable | plain | pretty | tight | ugly |
|--------|-------------|-------|--------|-------|------|

**A.  Nick:** Do you like these pants, Paul?

**Paul:** Well, I like the color. They're _____*bright*_____ .
                                                        1
  But . . .

**Nick:** But?

**Paul:** Um, well . . . Do they fit?

**Nick:** Actually, no. They're fairly _____ .
                                                        2

**Paul:** Why don't you try on a bigger size?

**Nick:** That's a good idea.

(Later)

**Nick:** OK. What do you think?

**Paul:** Those pants look good on you. And they look more _____ .
                                                        3

**B.  Mary:** Look at this dress, Paula. It's really _____ . I love it!
                                                        1

**Paula:** Well, I don't. It's just a black dress. It's very _____ .
                                                        2

**Mary:** I know, but it's nice.

**Paula:** Well, I don't think it's pretty. I think it's _____ .
                                                        3

**Mary:** Really? Now I don't want to buy it.

**3** Put the words in the correct order to make sentences.

1. isn't / This / enough / shirt / big / .    _This shirt isn't big enough._

2. clothes / have / He / doesn't / enough / . _____

3. is / My / tight / jacket / too / . _____

4. don't / enough / have / We / time / . _____

5. enough / Her / warm / coat / isn't / . _____

6. glasses / too / these / Are / expensive / ? _____

7. shoes / Do / enough / you / have / ? _____

8. this / cheap / Is / belt / enough / ? _____

**4** Complete the sentences with *too* or *enough*.

**A**

This blouse is _____*too*_____ big, and these pants
                     1
aren't long _____ ! The bag is _____
                2                              3
expensive, and the shoes are _____ tight.
                                    4

**B**

This jacket is _____ small, and these
                        1
pants are _____ baggy. The bag is
                 2
ugly, and the shoes aren't big _____ !
                                        3

**C**

This blouse isn't nice _____ , but I like the
                              1
pants. The bag isn't big _____ , and the
                                 2
shoes are _____ expensive. I don't have
                  3
_____ money. I hate shopping!
       4

**5** Match the pictures to the sentences from Exercise 4. Write A, B, or C.

1. ☐

2. ☐

3. ☐

**6** Write sentences in the simple present. Use the words in parentheses and *too* or *enough.*

1. _We don't have enough pasta._

   (we / not have / pasta)

2. _____

   (this sofa / not be / big)

3. _____

   (she / not be / tall)

4. _____

   (these pants / be / short)

5. _____

   (it / be / cold)

6. _____

   (there be / space / in the closet)

7. _____

   (he / not get / sleep)

8. _____

   (these weights / be / heavy)

# D A shopper's paradise

**1** Read the article. Then number the pictures.

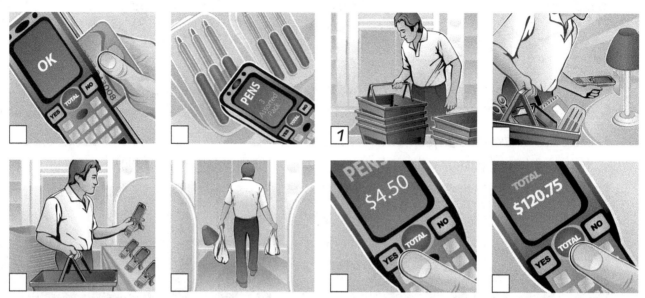

## Oh Office has a new way to shop.

### Come and try it! It's easier than shopping the old way.

**1.** Enter our store. Get a shopping basket. Our baskets are bigger than baskets in other stores. You have enough space for pencils, paper, small office lamps, and more!

**2.** Take a *go-scan* from the shelf next to the baskets. Turn it on.

**3.** Start shopping! Scan an item you want to buy.

**4.** Look at the price on the window of the *go-scan*. Do you want the item? Yes! Touch the "yes" button, and scan the item again. Then put it in your basket. You don't want the item? Touch the "no" button, and put the item back on the shelf.

**5.** Continue shopping and scanning!

**6.** Are you finished? Touch the "total" button on the *go-scan*. How much is it?

**7.** Put your credit card in the *go-scan*.

**8.** Put your things in a bag and go home.

**See you soon at Oh Office!**

**2** Read the article again. Then answer the questions.

1. What kind of store is it? _It's an office store._

2. Where are the *go-scans*? _____

3. Are Oh Office baskets smaller than baskets in other stores? _____

4. Which button is for items you want? _____

5. Which button shows how much everything costs? _____

# Fun in the city

## A  *You shouldn't miss it!*

**1**  Complete the captions under the pictures with the words in the box.

| | | | |
|---|---|---|---|
| Botanical Garden | Fountain | ✓Palace | Square |
| Castle | Monument | Pyramid | Statue |

1. Grand *Palace*

2. Trim _____

3. _____ of King Leonidas of Sparta

4. Chichen Itza Mayan _____

5. New York _____

6. Arc de Triomphe _____

7. Friendship of the Peoples _____

8. Federation _____

**2**  Complete the sentences. Write three of the places from Exercise 1.

1. The _____ is in the Park of Soviet Economic Achievement in Moscow.

2. The _____ is in Greece. It's bigger and taller than a real man.

3. The _____ is in Bangkok, Thailand. The queen and king live there sometimes.

**3** Complete the conversations with *should* or *shouldn't.*

A.     **Eva:** I'm going to Peru on vacation. Where _____*should*_____ I go?
                                                                    1

   **Simone:** You _____ go to Arequipa. It's beautiful. And
                                2

            you _____ miss Cuzco. It's amazing!
                        3

B.    **Cory:** I want to buy a CD. Where _____ I buy it?
                                                    1

      **Ben:** You _____ buy it at the mall. It's too expensive.
                          2

            You _____ buy it online. It's cheaper.
                        3

C. **Jung Ah:** How _____ we get to the restaurant?
                          1

   **Su Ho:** Well, we _____ take the bus. It's too slow.
                            2

   **Jung Ah:** _____ we take a taxi?
                      3

   **Su Ho:** Yes, we _____ .
                            4

D. **Andres:** What time _____ we come to your party?
                              1

   **Santos:** You _____ come early. You can help me with the food.
                        2

   **Andres:** _____ I come at 6:00?
                      3

   **Santos:** No, you _____ . That's too early. How about at 7:00?
                              4

   **Andres:** OK.

**4** Look at the weather information for each city. Then answer the questions.

| Cairo | Seoul | Chicago | Vancouver |

1. Mateo hates cold weather. Should he go to Cairo?          _*Yes, he should.*_____

2. Alison doesn't like rainy weather. Should she go to Seoul?    _____

3. Kyle and Casey want to ski. Should they go to Vancouver?    _____

4. I don't like hot weather. Should I go to Chicago?          _____

5. Paul wants to swim outside. Should he go to Vancouver?      _____

6. Mr. and Mrs. Willis like cold weather. Should they go to Cairo? _____

**5** Write sentences about Tours 1 and 2. Use *can* or *can't*.

# CITY TRAVEL

| | go to a museum | see a palace | visit a monument | have lunch at a castle |
|---|---|---|---|---|
| Tour 1 | ✗ | ✓ | ✗ | ✓ |
| Tour 2 | ✓ | ✗ | ✓ | ✗ |
| Tour 3 | ✗ | ✓ | ✓ | ✗ |
| Tour 4 | ✗ | ✓ | ✗ | ✓ |

1. On Tour 1, _you can't go to a museum_ or _____ .

   _You can see a palace_ and _____ .

2. On Tour 2, _____ or _____ .

   _____ and _____ .

**6** Answer the questions about Tours 3 and 4. Use the information from Exercise 5.

1. Can Susan go to a museum on Tour 3?    _No, she can't._ _____

2. Can we have lunch at a castle on Tour 4?    _____

3. Can you visit a monument on Tour 4?    _____

4. Can Jack see a palace on Tour 3?    _____

5. Can Jean and Paul go to a museum on Tour 4?    _____

**7** Circle the correct answer.

1. The main square is great! You _____ go there tomorrow.

   (a.) should    b. shouldn't    c. can't

2. There are 150 statues in this city. You _____ see them all in one day.

   a. should    b. can't    c. can

3. Julia loves to ski. She _____ go to Canada. There's a lot of snow there in the winter.

   a. should    b. can't    c. shouldn't

4. We _____ eat pasta. There's a good Italian restaurant across the street.

   a. shouldn't    b. can't    c. can

5. It's extremely hot today. We _____ take our coats on the tour.

   a. should    b. can    c. shouldn't

# B I'd recommend going . . .

**1** Write the lines of the conversation in the correct order.

> Almost, but I don't know much about Montpellier. What do you think I should do there?
> ✓Hi, Mari.
> I'd suggest seeing the botanical garden.
> Oh, hi, Ray. Are you ready for your trip to France?
> OK. That sounds good.
> Botanical garden?
> Yes. You can see all of the botanical garden in one day, and it's great.

Ray: _Hi, Mari._

Mari: _____

Ray: _____

Mari: _____

Ray: _____

Mari: _____

Ray: _____

**2** Write a conversation with the words and expressions in the box. Use Exercise 1 as a model.

> Italy
> Rome
> the fountains
> I'd recommend . . .
> What would you recommend doing there?

Lina: _Hi, Sergio._

Sergio: _____

Lina: _____

Sergio: _____

Lina: _____

Sergio: _____

Lina: _____

**1 Put the letters in the correct order to make adjectives.**

1. e d m o r n      _____*modern*_____
2. s s s e u t f r l      _____
3. g l u y      _____
4. n c e a l      _____
5. a t d a l o r i i t n      _____
6. l b f i e t a u u      _____
7. l x i a r g e n      _____
8. f a s e      _____
9. a o d u r n s e g      _____
10. i y d t r      _____

**2 Describe the pictures. Give your opinion. Use some of the words from Exercise 1.**

*Example:* __It's a beautiful and safe city.__

1. _____
   _____

2. _____
   _____

3. _____
   _____

4. _____
   _____

5. _____
   _____

6. _____
   _____

**3** **Rewrite the sentences with the opposite adjectives.**

1. It's the most modern hotel in the city.

   _It's the most traditional hotel in the city._

2. It's the safest city in the world.

   _____

3. It's the most beautiful restaurant in Chicago.

   _____

4. The bookstore is the most expensive store in the mall.

   _____

5. Shannon has the most stressful job in the world!

   _____

6. Market Street is the noisiest street in my town.

   _____

7. It's the cleanest beach in Spain.

   _____

8. It's the smallest café by the park.

   _____

**4** **Read the clues. Then answer the questions.**

1. • Miami is bigger than Naples.

   • Key Largo is smaller than Naples.

   What's the biggest city in Florida?    _Miami is the biggest city in Florida._

2. • Oliver is shorter than Ethan.

   • Matt is taller than Ethan.

   Who's the tallest boy in the class?    _____

3. • Main Street is dirtier than Elm Street.

   • Park Street is cleaner than Elm Street.

   What's the cleanest street in the town?    _____

4. • Jane's computer is newer than David's computer.

   • Wendy's computer is older than Jane's computer.

   Who has the newest computer in the family?    _____

**5** Complete the paragraphs with the superlative form of the adjectives in parentheses.

# What's your favorite place?

Posted by: **KateMonk12**

I love going to Thailand. Bangkok is

___the biggest___ (big) city in Thailand. I always stay in
<sub>1</sub>

_____ (clean) and _____ (safe)
<sub>2</sub> <sub>3</sub>

hotel in the city. It's also close to the markets. I get

_____ (beautiful) clothes there!
<sub>4</sub>

Posted by: **DavidP**

Sometimes I think I have _____ (bad) and
<sub>5</sub>

_____ (stressful) job in the world! But, not always.
<sub>6</sub>

I sometimes travel for work, and it's great. My favorite place is a hotel

in San Diego. The pool is _____ (relaxing) place! But
<sub>7</sub>

it's not my favorite place in the hotel. I love the hotel restaurant. I think it's

one of _____ (good) restaurants in the city.
<sub>8</sub>

Posted by: **LivLiv**

My favorite city is Tokyo. It's _____ (modern) city
<sub>9</sub>

in Japan. I think it's _____ (clean) big city in the world.
<sub>10</sub>

I like visiting the Tokyo National Museum. It's _____
<sub>11</sub>

(old) museum in Japan, and it's also one of _____
<sub>12</sub>

(traditional).

**6** Answer the questions with information about your country.

1. What's the oldest city? _____

2. What's the best season to travel? _____

3. What's the coldest city? _____

4. What's the hottest city? _____

5. Where's the biggest park? _____

6. What's the most modern museum? _____

# D The best place to go

**1** **Read the blog. Then circle the correct answer.**

1. *Eating a Biscuit Together* is by **Ku BomJu** / **Bukchon**.

2. The statue of the businessman is in **Los Angeles** / **Ernst & Young**.

3. The statue in Australia is a statue of Charles **La Trobe** / **Robb**.

4. The artist of *The Runner* is Costas **Dromeas** / **Varotsos**.

# Unusual Statues around the World

I travel a lot for work and for fun. I see a lot of famous landmarks.
*The Statue of Liberty* in New York City is my favorite statue, but
here are some unusual statues from my travels.

This statue is called *Eating a Biscuit Together*. This statue is actually a bench – you can sit on it! It's by artist Ku BomJu, and it's in front of the Bukchon Art Museum in Seoul, Korea. I think it's very funny!

I don't know the artist or name of this statue, but I really like it! It's a statue of a businessman in Los Angeles, California. It's in front of the Ernst & Young Building. I think he has the most stressful job in Los Angeles. Maybe he is an accountant for a movie star!

 You can't miss this statue! It's of Charles La Trobe, a famous politician in Australia in the 1800s. The artist's name is Charles Robb. It's at La Trobe University Bundoora in Melbourne, Australia. Do you think his head hurts?

I love this statue! It's called *Dromeas II*, but people call it *The Runner* in English. It has a lot of glass plates that make the shape of a runner. The artist is Costas Varotsos. It's in front of the Athens Hilton hotel in Athens, Greece. I think it's the fastest statue in the world, but it's not going far!

**2** **Read the article again. Write T (true), F (false), or NI (no information).**

1. The Bukchon Art Museum has traditional Korean art. ___*NI*___

2. The statue of the businessman is in Europe. _____

3. The statue in Australia doesn't have a head. _____

4. The statue *The Runner* is in Greece. _____

5. *The Runner* is the writer's favorite statue. _____

# People

## A   *Where was he born?*

**1** Look at the pictures. Complete the puzzle with career words.

 1.

 2.

 3.

 4.

 5.

 6.

 7.

 8.

**2 Rewrite the sentences. Use the past of *be* and the words in parentheses.**

1. I'm in Chicago right now.

   <u>I was in Chicago last week</u>_____ . (last week)

2. Tom and Carol are at a basketball game tonight.

   _____ . (last night)

3. Where are you right now?

   _____ ? (yesterday)

4. Stephanie and Kim aren't in class today.

   _____ . (on Tuesday)

5. Is David at the party tonight?

   _____ ? (on Friday night)

6. Tameka isn't tired now.

   _____ . (in the morning)

**3 Look at the chart. Then answer the questions.**

| Family name | First name | Title | Birthday | Place of birth |
|---|---|---|---|---|
| Balkan | Erol | Mr. | January 17, 1992 | Istanbul |
| Davis | Cassandra | Ms. | April 7, 1986 | San Francisco |
| Ferris | Alicia | Mrs. | December 10, 1950 | Vancouver |
| Gomez | Rodrigo | Mr. | June 4, 1975 | Mexico City |
| Johnson | Kyle | Mr. | May 23, 1986 | Melbourne |
| Kato | Sakura | Mrs. | January 18, 1967 | Tokyo |
| Morgan | Wendy | Ms. | October 8, 1974 | Vancouver |

1. Where was Erol born?   <u>He was born in Istanbul.</u>_____

2. When was Alicia born?   _____

3. Was Sakura born in Tokyo?   _____

4. Was Rodrigo born in July?   _____

5. Were Cassandra and Kyle born in 1988?   _____

6. Where were Alicia and Wendy born?   _____

7. Were Erol and Sakura born in January?   _____

8. When was Rodrigo born?   _____

**4** Complete the conversation with the correct form of the past of *be*.

Jay: Hey, Shelly. This is really interesting . . .

Shelly: What?

Jay: Well, I'm reading about Leonardo da Vinci.

Shelly: Oh. _____*Was*_____ he an explorer?
                  1

Jay: No, he _____ . He _____ a famous artist. Many
                          2                           3

of his paintings _____ famous, such as the *Mona Lisa.*
                             4

Shelly: Oh, yeah. That's right.

Jay: But I didn't know this. He _____ also a musician and a writer!
                                  5

Shelly: Wow. _____ he born in Italy?
                 6

Jay: Yes, he _____ . He _____ born in Vinci,
                   7                       8

a small town in Italy.

Shelly: Vinci, like his last name.

Jay: Yes, "da Vinci" means "from Vinci." Hey, he _____ born on
                                      9

April 15, 1452. That's your birthday!

Shelly: No, it isn't. I _____ born on April 15. My birthday is April 16.
                        10

Jay: Oh, yeah. Well, listen to this. He _____ also a great scientist
                                    11

with many inventions.

Shelly: _____ his inventions popular?
          12

Jay: No, they _____ . And the technology _____
                  13                           14

available then to make his inventions.

**5** Answer the questions with your own information.

1. Where were you born? _____

2. When were you born? _____

3. When were your parents born? _____

4. Where were you yesterday afternoon? _____

5. Were you in your English class yesterday? _____

# B  I'm not sure, but I think . . .

**1** Complete the expressions of certainty and uncertainty in the conversation.

**Jerry:** Hey, Tanya, can you help me with this puzzle?

**Tanya:** Sure.

**Jerry:** Who was Coco Chanel?

**Tanya:** She was a famous designer.

**Jerry:** Are you sure?

**Tanya:** I'm p_____ .
                              1

**Jerry:** OK. D-E-S . . . Yes, that's an eight-letter word. It works! And what was the last name of the Mexican president in 2002?

**Tanya:** I'm not s_____ , but I think it
                              2
was Fox.

**Jerry:** Yes, that works. Oh, I know this one. Mozart's first name was Wolfgang.

**Tanya:** Are you sure? I think it was Ludwig.

**Jerry:** No, it wasn't Ludwig. I'm c_____
                                        3
it was Wolfgang. It has eight letters.

**2** Complete the conversation with expressions of certainty or uncertainty. More than one answer is possible.

**Jerry:** OK. Only three more. Who is Elena Ochoa?

**Tanya:** I'm _____ , but I think she was
                              1
a scientist.

**Jerry:** Hmm . . . That doesn't fit. It starts with an *A* . . . I know, she was an astronaut!

**Tanya:** Are you sure?

**Jerry:** Yes. _____ ! OK. This one's difficult. Who
                              2
was Eiji Sawamura?

**Tanya:** _____ , but I think he was a soccer player.
                              3
No, wait, he was a baseball player! _____ .
                                                              4

**Jerry:** You're right. Thanks!

# C  *People I admire*

**1** Complete the sentences in the evaluations with the words in the box.

| brave | caring | determined | honest | inspiring | intelligent | passionate | talented |
|---|---|---|---|---|---|---|---|

## TOMKINS ACCOUNTING

**Name:** _Orlando Rodriguez_   **Position:** _Accountant_

**Overall rating:** _Very good_

**Comments:**

Orlando is extremely _____. He learns new things quickly and easily.
<br>1

He's also very _____. He tries everything possible to do a good job.
<br>2

He's always on time, and he's very _____. He always tells the truth,
<br>3

even when others don't agree with his opinion.

## Perfect Pets Animal Care

**Name:** _Josie Kennedy_   **Position:** _Assistant_

**Notes:**

I think Josie is good for the job. She is very _____. She was nice to all
<br>4

the animals here. She's also very _____. She wasn't afraid to work
<br>5

with the bigger dogs. I recommend Josie for this job.

## LTC Teamwork Presentation

**Overall rating:** ☑ Very good  ☐ Good  ☐ Not good

**Comments:**

The presentation on teamwork was very good. I learned a lot about how to work with people

in groups. Ms. Beck was a great teacher. She was very _____ about
<br>6

teamwork and showed strong feelings about it. She was _____, and
<br>7

now I want to do more teamwork with people at my office! She's also a

_____ writer. She's very good at writing how-to books. I want to buy
<br>8

her newest book.

**2** Complete the email. Use the simple past of the verbs in parentheses.

TO: Bob@email.com

Hello from San Diego!

I'm having a great vacation! It's very warm here.

Yesterday we _____*went*_____ (go) to Balboa Park. It's a really big
                      1
park, so we _____ (decide) to stay all day. In the park,
                    2
we _____ (visit) the San Diego Zoo. It's the biggest zoo
              3
in California! After that, we _____ (walk) around other
                                        4
parts of the park, and we _____ (get) really tired. But we
                                    5
_____ (see) some beautiful fountains and statues, and
          6
my brother _____ (meet) a movie star!
                    7

We _____ (eat) lunch at a café in the park. We
              8
_____ (have) some good sandwiches, but my parents
          9
_____ (not like) them.
          10

See you soon!

Terri

**3** Write questions with the words in parentheses and the simple past. Then answer the questions with the information in Exercise 1.

1. A: _Where did Terri go on vacation_____ ? (Where / Terri / go / on vacation)

   B: _She went to San Diego_____ .

2. A: Did _____ ? (Terri / go / to the park with her family)

   B: _____ .

3. A: _____ ? (What / they / visit / in the park)

   B: _____ .

4. A: _____ ? (they / get / tired)

   B: _____ .

5. A: _____ ? (Where / they / eat / lunch)

   B: _____ .

6. A: _____ ? (Terri's parents / like / the food)

   B: _____ .

**4** Look at Miguel's status updates. Then write sentences about his week. Use the simple past and *ago*.

# SOCIALSPACE

## Miguel Trandall

**STATUS UPDATES**

I'm eating fish at a Thai restaurant. Yum! 🙂
*Posted on Monday, 4/12 at 2:40 p.m.*

Miranda and I are shopping.
*Posted on Tuesday, 4/13 at 7:32 p.m.*

I'm watching a boring reality show. 🙁
*Posted on Wednesday, 4/14 at 9:05 p.m.*

I'm not going to the park. It's too cold!
*Posted on Thursday, 4/15 at 5:15 p.m.*

My mom and I are eating breakfast in a coffee shop.
*Posted on Friday, 4/16 at 8:10 a.m.*

Martin and I are lifting weights. Ugh!
*Posted on Saturday, 4/17 at 11:23 a.m.*

My sister and I aren't going out. We're too tired!
*Posted on Sunday, 4/18 at 12:00 p.m.*

Today is Monday, 4/19.

1. *Miguel ate fish at a Thai restaurant seven days ago.*

2. _____

3. _____

4. _____

5. _____

6. _____

7. _____

**1** Read the article. Then check (✓) the adjectives that describe each person.

|  | brave | determined | inspiring | passionate | talented |
|---|---|---|---|---|---|
| 1. John Muir |  |  | ✓ |  |  |
| 2. Ada Blackjack |  |  |  |  |  |
| 3. Louis Armstrong |  |  |  |  |  |

## Book Corner
Books in review this week: <u>Biographies</u>                **BOOK**MAGAZINE

*A Passion for Nature: The Life of John Muir* by Donald Worster

This biography about John Muir was terrific. John Muir was born in Scotland in 1838, and he moved to the United States in 1849. He was an explorer and a writer, and he was a very inspiring person. He was passionate about nature, and he helped to create many national parks in the United States. In this book, Donald Worster describes Muir's inspiring travel and work. He also writes about Muir's life with his family and friends.

*Ada Blackjack: A True Story of Survival in the Arctic* by Jennifer Nevin

Ada Blackjack was born in 1898 in Alaska. In 1921, she went with one Canadian and three American explorers to Wrangel Island in the Arctic. The four men wanted to explore the island. Ada was their cook. After two years, they didn't have enough food and had to leave the island. One man was too sick to travel. Three of the men left to find help. Ada stayed with the sick man. After three months, the man died. Then Ada was alone on the island. She was there for five months, but Ada was determined and brave. Finally, a search team found her, and Ada went back to Alaska. It's an exciting book, and Jennifer Nevin tells Ada's story very well.

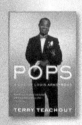

*Pops: A Life of Louis Armstrong* by Terry Teachout

Louis Armstrong was born in New Orleans in 1901. He was an extremely talented jazz musician, composer, and singer. He influenced all kinds of musicians and singers, including jazz and pop musicians and singers who are popular today. Louis Armstrong was famous all over the world. In 2001, one hundred years after his birth, the New Orleans airport was renamed Louis Armstrong International Airport in his honor. Terry Teachout writes about Armstrong's music, but he also writes about his life. He shows that Louis Armstrong was an inspiring musician who had an extremely interesting life.

**2** Read the article again. Answer the questions.

1. Where was John Muir born?          *He was born in Scotland.*

2. When did Muir move to the United States?  _____

3. When did Ada Blackjack go to Wrangel Island? _____

4. How long was Blackjack alone on the island? _____

5. Where was Louis Armstrong born?      _____

6. What was Armstrong's job?          _____

# In a restaurant

## The ice cream is fantastic!

**1** Cross out the words that don't belong in each list.

1. **Main dishes:**  chicken stir-fry    ~~fruit salad~~    lamb chop    cheese ravioli

2. **Desserts:**  apple pie    ice cream    cheesecake    steak

3. **Side dishes:**  mashed potatoes    French fries    mixed vegetables    tomato soup

4. **Appetizer:**  crab cakes    garlic bread    rice    onion rings

**2** Label the food with some of the menu items from Exercise 1.

1. _____

2. _____

3. _____

4. _____

5. _____

6. _____

7. _____

8. _____

9. _____

10. _____

**3** Plan a party. Write menu items for each category. Use your own ideas.

**PARTY MENU**

Appetizers:
_____
_____

Main dishes:
_____
_____

Side dishes:
_____
_____
_____

Desserts:
_____
_____

**4** Circle the correct word in the parentheses at the end of the sentence to complete each conversation.

1. **A:** How are the desserts? Any recommendations?

   **B:** I had _____ apple pie. It's great! (an / a / the)

2. **A:** Let's order _____ garlic bread. (some / a / an)

   **B:** Not for me, thanks. I don't like garlic.

3. **A:** Let's try _____ appetizer! (some / a / an)

   **B:** OK.

4. **A:** Do you want coffee?

   **B:** Yes, please. With _____ milk. (some / the / a)

5. **A:** What do you want for dinner?

   **B:** I think I'll start with _____ dessert! (an / a / the)

6. **A:** Do you want _____ cheese ravioli? (an / a / some)

   **B:** No, thank you.

**5** Look at the pictures. Complete the sentences with the names of the people having the food. Then circle the correct words to complete the sentences.

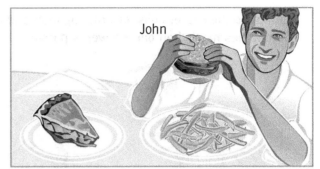

1. _____*John*_____ is having **a** / **some** hamburger, **the** / **some** French fries, and **the** / **some** apple pie.

2. _____ is having **a** / **some** garlic bread, **the** / **some** cheese ravioli, and **a** / **some** cheesecake.

3. _____ is having **a** / **some** steak, **a** / **some** mashed potatoes, and **the** / **some** ice cream.

4. _____ is having **the** / **some** chicken soup, **a** / **the** hot dog, and **a** / **an** fruit salad.

**6** Complete the conversations with *a / an*, *the*, or *some*.

**A. Randy:** What did you have for lunch today?

    **Joe:** I had _____*a*_____ hot dog and _____ tomato soup.
                                1                        2

    **Randy:** How were they?

    **Joe:** _____ hot dog was very good, but _____ soup was cold.
                3                          4

**B. David:** What did you have?

    **Marcia:** I had _____ garlic bread and _____ cheese ravioli.
                            1                        2

    **David:** How were they?

    **Marcia:** _____ garlic bread and _____ cheese ravioli were good.
                 3                        4

## B I'll have the fish, please.

**1** Complete the expressions for ordering food and checking information.
Sometimes more than one answer is possible.

**Waiter:** Are you ready to order?

**Joshua:** Yes, I am.

**Waiter:** OK. What would you like?

**Joshua:** I'll _____**have**_____ the chicken
          1
stir-fry and some rice, please.

**Waiter:** Anything else?

**Joshua:** No, thank you.

**Waiter:** OK. Let me _____ that.
                           2
You'd like the chicken stir-fry and some
rice.

**Joshua:** Yes. Oh, and I'd _____
                              3
some onion soup, too.

**Waiter:** Is that all?

**Joshua:** Yes, that's all.

**Waiter:** OK. Let me _____ that.
                          4
You'd like the chicken stir-fry, some rice,
and some onion soup.

**Joshua:** That's right. Oh, wait! Can I

_____ some water,
        5
please?

**Waiter:** Sure. Is that all?

**Joshua:** Yes. Thank you.

**Waiter:** Let me _____ that
                      6
back. The chicken stir-fry, some rice, some
onion soup, and some water.

**Joshua:** Yes, please. That's all, thank you!

**2** Complete the conversation with your own ideas and the expressions in Exercise 1.

**Waiter:** Are you ready to order?

**You:** Yes. _____

**Waiter:** Anything else?

**You:** Um, yes. _____

**Waiter:** OK. Let me _____

**You:** That's right. Thank you.

# C Have you ever...?

**1** Put the letters in the correct order to make food words.

1. a a o c s o v d  _____avocados_____
2. y s o e t s r  _____
3. a s d e t  _____
4. i d s u q  _____
5. a e s d e w e  _____

6. n a s p i n l t a  _____
7. y s o  l m i k  _____
8. a r c o r t  u j e i c  _____
9. l b e u  e h e c s e  _____
10. z f e o n r  g o u t y r  _____

**2** Complete the order form from an online supermarket. Use some words from Exercise 1.

| FOOD MART | | |
|---|---|---|
| | **Item** | **Price** |
| | 1. _____avocados_____ | $0.98 |
| | 2. _____ | $4.25 |
| | 3. _____ | $5.00 |
| | 4. _____ | $1.56 |
| | 5. _____ | $4.75 |
| | 6. _____ | $3.89 |
| | 7. _____ | $6.20 |
| | 8. _____ | $3.42 |

**3** Complete the chart with the correct past participles.

| Verb | Past participle |
| --- | --- |
| 1. be | *been* |
| 2. drink | |
| 3. eat | |
| 4. have | |
| 5. try | |

**4** Look at Ramiro's answers to the quiz. Then write sentences about Ramiro's food experiences. Use the present perfect.

## ARE YOU AN ADVENTUROUS EATER?

**Answer the questions.**

1. How many times have you eaten black spaghetti?  ten times

2. Have you ever drunk seaweed juice?  ○ Yes  ● No

3. Have you ever tried squid?  ● Yes  ○ No

4. How often have you had unusual food?  many times

5. Have you ever eaten plantains?  ● Yes  ○ No

6. Have you ever had fish tacos?  ○ Yes  ● No

7. Have you been to restaurants in other countries?  ● Yes  ○ No

8. How often have you cooked unusual foods at home?  never

**RESULTS:** You are a fairly adventurous eater.

1.  *Ramiro has eaten black spaghetti ten times.*
2.  *He has never drunk seaweed juice.*
3.  _____
4.  _____
5.  _____
6.  _____
7.  _____
8.  _____

**5** Complete the conversation. Use the present perfect and the words in parentheses.

**Mark:** Hey, Vince. *Have you ever eaten* (eat) oysters?
                                    1

**Vince:** No, I _____ . Have you ever
                          2
eaten them?

**Mark:** Yes, I _____ . They're delicious!
                          3

**Vince:** _____ (be) to
                              4
the Seascape Restaurant?

**Mark:** No, I _____ . Is it good?
                        5

**Vince:** Yeah, it's great! My wife and I

_____ (eat) there three times.
              6

**Mark:** _____ (have) the seafood there?
                            7

**Vince:** Um, no, I _____ . I usually have the chicken!
                          8

**Mark:** Really?

**Vince:** Yes. But people say the oysters are fantastic.


**6** Read the answers. Write the questions.

1. *Have you ever tried squid sushi?*     No, I haven't. I've never tried squid sushi.

2. _____     Yes, I have. I've had chicken tacos many times.

3. _____     Yes, I have. I've drunk carrot juice before.

    No, I haven't. I've never been to a Colombian

4. _____     restaurant.

5. _____     No, I haven't. I've never eaten plantains.

    Yes, I have. I've been to Chinese restaurants

6. _____     many times.


**7** Answer the questions in Exercise 6 with your own information. Write a short
answer and add a sentence. Use the sentences in Exercise 6 as models.

1. _____    _____

2. _____    _____

3. _____    _____

4. _____    _____

5. _____    _____

6. _____    _____

## D | Restaurant experiences

**1** Read the webpage. How many seafood items are on the menu?

There are _____ seafood items on the menu.

### YOUR MENU  Find a restaurant near you!

| New Search | Profile and Reviews | Menu |
|---|---|---|

**New Search**

**by rating**
★
★★
★★★
★★★★

**by price**
$
$$
$$$

**by type of food**
American
Chinese
Colombian
Korean
Mexican
Turkish
Vietnamese

cafés
sandwiches
seafood
traditional
vegetarian

**Profile and Reviews**

### Sun Seafood and Son

**Food:** ★ ★ ★ ★
**Price:** $$
**Website:** www.sss/cup.com
**Hours:** 12:30 p.m.–10:00 p.m.
Monday–Friday

9:00 a.m.–10:00 p.m.
Saturday–Sunday

**Reviews**

*Posted by RickN on 4/27*
The food at this restaurant is delicious! I recommend the crab cakes with blue cheese for an appetizer. I also like the mixed seafood salad. My favorite main dish is the squid stir-fry! All of the seafood is good.

*Posted by Carla82 on 5/16*
This restaurant is pretty good. I liked the seafood, but I didn't like the juices. I recommend getting water to drink!

*Posted by Jake on 6/2*
This is the best restaurant in this city. I've had everything on the menu! The side dishes are delicious. Try the mixed vegetables with crab. Oh, and have dessert. The seaweed ice cream is delicious! It really is!

**Menu**

**Appetizers:**
crab cakes with blue
cheese
onion soup
mixed seafood salad

**Main dishes:**
squid stir-fry
fish of the day
seafood ravioli

**Side dishes:**
mixed vegetables
with crab
rice
fried mushrooms

**Drinks:**
carrot juice
seaweed tea
water

**Desserts:**
cheesecake
seaweed ice cream
fruit salad

**2** Read the article again. Check (✓) the items that are definitely true.

☐ RickN liked the crab cakes.

☐ RickN has only tried three items on the menu.

☐ Carla82 tried some juice at the restaurant.

☐ Carla82 does not like seaweed.

☐ Jake has never eaten a main dish at the restaurant.

☐ Jake liked the ice cream.

# Entertainment

## A  *I'm not a fan of dramas.*

**1**  Look at the pictures. Circle the correct type of movie to label each picture.

1. a. a science-fiction movie
   b. an action movie

2. a. a comedy
   b. a horror movie

3. a. a horror movie
   b. a musical

4. a. an animated movie
   b. a science-fiction movie

5. a. a western
   b. a comedy

6. a. a drama
   b. a comedy

7. a. an action movie
   b. an animated movie

8. a. a western
   b. a musical

**2** Respond to the statements. Complete the sentences with *so* or *neither* and *am* or *do*.

1. **A:** I love horror movies!

   **B:** _So do_ I.

2. **A:** I'm not a fan of musicals.

   **B:** _____ I.

3. **A:** I never go to the movies on Sundays.

   **B:** _____ I.

4. **A:** I'm really tired.

   **B:** _____ I.

5. **A:** I have a lot of homework tonight.

   **B:** _____ I.

6. **A:** I don't like seafood.

   **B:** _____ I.

**3** Rewrite the responses in Exercise 2 using *too* or *either*.

1. **A:** I love horror movies!

   **B:** _I do, too._

2. **A:** I'm not a fan of musicals.

   **B:** _____

3. **A:** I never go to the movies on Sundays.

   **B:** _____

4. **A:** I'm really tired.

   **B:** _____

5. **A:** I have a lot of homework tonight.

   **B:** _____

6. **A:** I don't like seafood.

   **B:** _____

**4** Circle the correct words to complete the conversations.

1. A: (I like) / I don't like tacos.

   B: So do I.

2. A: I like / I don't like westerns.

   B: I don't, either.

3. A: I'm / I'm not a fan of science fiction movies.

   B: Really? I am. I love them!

4. A: I'm always / I'm never on time.

   B: Neither am I.

5. A: I'm / I'm not cold!

   B: I am, too.

6. A: I eat / I don't eat a lot of pizza.

   B: Really? I don't. I hardly ever eat pizza.

**5** Complete the conversations with your own responses.

1. A: I'm not a fan of horror movies.

   You: _Neither am I._ or _Really? I am. I like horror movies._

2. A: I love doing laundry.

   You: _____

3. A: I always get up late on Saturdays.

   You: _____

4. A: I don't usually eat a big breakfast in the morning.

   You: _____

5. A: I'm not a fan of action movies.

   You: _____

6. A: I'm usually late for class.

   You: _____

# B Any suggestions?

**1** Put the words in the correct order to make expressions to ask for and give suggestions.

1. suggestions / Any / ?        _Any suggestions?_

2. any / you / suggestions / Do / have / ?        _____

3. an / see / movie / action / Let's / .        _____

4. a / we / Why / movie / don't / to / go / ?        _____

5. you / suggest / What / do / ?        _____

6. TV / could / We / watch / .        _____

**2** Complete the conversation with the sentences from Exercise 1. Use each sentence once.

**Ivan:** So, what do you want to do today?

**Emily:** I don't know. _Do you have any suggestions_ ?
<br>¹

**Ivan:** _____ .
<br>²

**Emily:** Sorry. I don't really want to watch TV.

**Ivan:** OK. _____ ?
<br>³

**Emily:** _____ ?
<br>⁴

**Ivan:** Good idea. What type of movie do you want to see?

**Emily:** Hmm, I don't know. _____ ?
<br>⁵

**Ivan:** Yes. _____ .
<br>⁶

**Emily:** That sounds good. There's a new action movie with Matt Damon.

**Ivan:** Great!

**3** Complete the conversations with your own suggestions.

1. **Friend:** I'd like to have something nice for dinner. Any suggestions?

   **You:** _____

2. **Friend:** I want do something different tonight. Do you have any suggestions?

   **You:** _____

3. **Friend:** I want to watch a good drama. What do you suggest?

   **You:** _____

## C  All of us love music.

**1** Look at the music calendar. Complete the words for the types of music.

# SWEET SOUND
### Café and Club

**Monday, 8:00 p.m.**

Listen to p _op_____ singer Laura Bee. She's singing, and

DJ Strong is playing t_____ music. Don't miss it!

**Tuesday, 9:30 p.m.**

Tuesday is b_____ night. Listen to Elsa Ford sing her

sad songs.

**Wednesday, 10:00 p.m.**

Do you prefer a quiet evening? Then stay home on Wednesday night!
The music is going to be loud. Listen to Heavy Sushi play

r_____ music.

**Thursday, 7:00 p.m.**

Melinda May is a great co_____ singer from Texas. Listen

to her new songs Thursday night.

**Friday, 7:00 p.m., 9:00 p.m.**

Listen to the best j_____ music in town. Monty Miles

plays twice!

**Saturday, 8:30 p.m.**

On Saturday night, r_____ musicians Kipp and Kyle play their

cool instruments, and h_____ star Bee Cool sings with them.

**Sunday, 2:00 p.m., 7:00 p.m.**

Do you like slow, quiet music? Lydia Saad sings f_____ songs

at lunch. At night, Daniel Avilez plays beautiful cl_____ music

on his guitar.

**2** Put the words in the correct place in the chart.

| ✓all of | a lot of | most of | none of | not many of | some of |

all of _____

_____

_____

_____

_____

_____

**3** Look at the survey. Then circle the correct answers to complete the sentences.

# What kind of music do you like?
We asked 100 students, and here are their answers.

| Type of music | Yes | No | Type of music | Yes | No |
|---|---|---|---|---|---|
| classical | 14 | 86 | jazz | 23 | 77 |
| rock | 82 | 18 | blues | 38 | 62 |
| pop | 100 | 0 | country | 8 | 92 |
| reggae | 35 | 65 | hip-hop | 95 | 5 |
| folk | 0 | 100 | techno | 86 | 14 |

1. (**Not many of** )/ **Most of** the students like classical music.

2. **All of** / **A lot of** them like rock music.

3. **All of** / **None of** them like pop music.

4. **Not many of** / **Some of** them like reggae.

5. **All of** / **None of** them like folk.

6. **A lot of** / **Not many of** them like jazz.

7. **All of** / **Some of** them like blues music.

8. **Not many of** / **None of** them like country.

9. **Some of** / **Most of** them like hip-hop.

10. **All of** / **A lot of** them like techno music.

**4** Look at the picture. Then rewrite the sentences to correct the underlined mistakes.

1. <u>Some of</u> the runners are tired.  *Many of the runners are tired.*

2. <u>None of</u> them are running.  _____

3. <u>Many of</u> them are sitting.  _____

4. <u>Most of</u> them are running fast.  _____

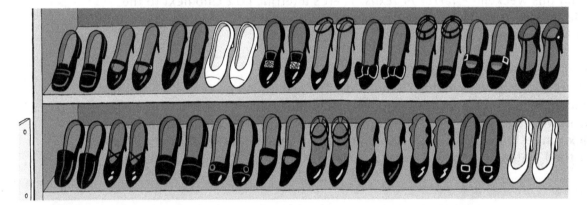

5. <u>All of</u> the shoes are black.  _____

6. <u>Many of</u> them are white.  _____

7. <u>A lot of</u> them are gray.  _____

8. <u>None of</u> the people are listening to music.  _____

9. <u>Not many of</u> them are reading.  _____

10. <u>Most of</u> them are sitting.  _____

# D Musicians from around the world

**1** Read the webpage. What four things does Mark like? Which one doesn't anyone write about?

Mark likes _____ .

None of them write about _____ .

---

**Posted by Mark at 6:15**

Hi! I'm new to this town. What can I do for fun this weekend? I like listening to music, eating at restaurants, and going to museums. I also love going to the movies! Any suggestions? Thanks for your help.

**Posted by Dennis102 at 6:18**

Hey, Mark. Welcome to our town. It's small, but it's great. There's a movie theater downtown on Maple Street. Do you like scary movies? There's a great horror movie playing this weekend – *Terror in Texas*. There's a terrific jazz club next to the movie theater. They have different musicians every weekend. A lot of them are from New Orleans.

**Posted by SandraMN at 6:32**

Hi, Mark. Do you have children? *Trudy Goes to Paris* is also playing. It's a terrific animated movie. There are a lot of good restaurants here. All of them are downtown. You can eat food from around the world. There's a Chinese restaurant, a Mexican restaurant, a Turkish restaurant, and a Vietnamese restaurant. Have you ever tried Vietnamese food? They play great folk music at this restaurant, too.

**Posted by LeroyLee at 6:45**

Welcome to our town, Mark! Sandra's recommendation is good. The food at the Vietnamese restaurant is delicious! My favorite place to hear music is Club 64. They usually have musicians from all over the world. This weekend Farah Fields is singing. She's a great blues singer. And next week, a rock band from England is playing.

**Posted by Mark at 6:59**

Thanks, everyone! I want to try the Vietnamese restaurant, and my wife and I will go to Club 64 next week. We love rock music! OK, I'm in a hurry . . . We're going to see *Terror in Texas* at 7:30! Thanks!

---

**2** Read the article again. Answer the questions.

1. Where is the jazz club? _next to the movie theater_

2. Where are a lot of the jazz musicians from? _____

3. Who recommends an animated movie? _____

4. What kinds of music are recommended? _____

# Time for a change

## A Personal change

**1** Complete the conversations with the phrases from the box.

| | | |
|---|---|---|
| get a credit card | lose weight | save money |
| join a gym | make more friends | start a new hobby |
| learn an instrument | ✓pass a test | study harder |

**A.** **Jake:** So, Wendy. What are you doing these days?

**Wendy:** Oh, I'm studying a lot to _pass a test_ .
<br>1

**Jake:** That's great! But why are you shopping right now?

**Wendy:** I don't know. I think I should go home

and _____ !
<br>2

**B. Doug:** Hey, Akio. Do you want to go to the movies?

**Akio:** No. It's too expensive. I'm trying to _____ .
<br>1

I want to _____ .
<br>2

**Doug:** Really? Why? Do you want to _____ ?
<br>3

**Akio:** Not really. I just want to exercise more.

**C.** **Mick:** Hey, Brenda. How can I _____ ?
<br>1

**Brenda:** Oh, it's easy. You can go online. But why do you want a

credit card?

**Mick:** I want to _____ , so I'm going to take
<br>2

guitar lessons!

**Brenda:** That's cool!

**Mick:** Yeah. But now I need to buy a guitar!

**D. Jen:** I'd like to do something different. Any suggestions?

**Ted:** Why don't you _____ , like taking pictures?
<br>1

**Jen:** Well, I have a camera, but I'm not very good at using it.

**Ted:** You could take a class. That's also a good way

to _____ .
<br>2

**Jen:** Yeah, thanks. That's a good idea.

**2** Put the words in the correct order to make sentences.

1. house / a / saving / buy / We're / money / to / new / .

   _We're saving money to buy a new house._

2. get / English / better job / Are / a / learning / you / to / ?

   _____

3. new friends / to / Lisa / gym / joined / a / make / .

   _____

4. movies / see / went / to / comedy / Ethan and Ruben / to / the / a / .

   _____

5. take / to / yoga / relax / I / classes / .

   _____

6. a / buy / more clothes / credit / Rita / Is / getting / card / to / ?

   _____

**3** Look at the chart. Why are the people taking the classes? Write sentences with the present continuous and infinitives of purpose.

## TEAM TIME SPORTS CENTER

| Name | Exercise / Class | Purpose / Goal |
|---|---|---|
| Kim Rawlings | take soccer lessons | play better |
| Ed Hendricks | lift weights | get stronger |
| Jim Franklin | take a salsa class | dance better |
| Hannah Park | take yoga | relax |
| Tina Madding | do gymnastics | have fun |
| Josh Sparks | learn karate | lose weight |

1. _Kim is taking soccer lessons to play better._

2. _____

3. _____

4. _____

5. _____

6. _____

**4** Complete the flyer. Write sentences with the words in parentheses. Use the imperative and infinitives of purpose.

## One-on-One ENGLISH

**Do you want to improve your English? Here are six easy ways.**

1. *Study harder to get better grades.* (study harder / get better grades)
2. _____ (take a writing class / improve your writing)
3. _____ (talk to English speakers / improve your pronunciation)
4. _____ (listen to music in English / improve your listening)
5. _____ (read websites in English / learn new words)
6. _____ (email Kate / take an English class)

**Kate Harrison: kateH@cup.org**   *Classes start every Monday.*

**5** Read the conversations. Complete the sentence about each person. Use infinitives of purpose.

1. **Julia:** Why are you going to Peru?

   **Lynn:** Because I want to see Machu Picchu.

   Lynn  *is going to Peru to see Machu Picchu.* _____

2. **Paul:** Why did you join a gym?

   **Doug:** Because I want to lose weight.

   Doug _____

3. **Wesley:** Why are you saving money?

   **Sandra:** Because I want to buy a car.

   Sandra _____

4. **Jill:** Why did you start an English club?

   **Tom:** Because I want to make more friends.

   Tom _____

**6** Answer the questions with your own information. Use infinitives of purpose.

*Example:*  *I'd like to visit Japan to see the botanical gardens.*

1. What country would you like to visit? Why? _____

2. What famous person would you like to meet? Why? _____

3. Why are you taking English classes? _____

4. What other language would you like to learn? Why? _____

# B  *I'm happy to hear that!*

**1** **Write the lines of the conversation in the correct order.**

> I'm good, thanks. But I had the flu last month.
> I'm sorry to hear that!
> Oh, hi, Ken. How are you doing?
> ✓ Hey, Sam. Long time no see.
> That's great to hear!
> That's wonderful! Have a great time!
> Yeah. And guess what? I'm going to Paris on Saturday.
> Yeah. I was sick for two weeks, but I feel better now.

Ken: *Hey, Sam. Long time no see.* _____

Sam: _____

Ken: _____

Sam: _____

Ken: _____

Sam: _____

Ken: _____

Sam: _____

**2** **Complete the conversations with the words in the box. Use each expression once.**
**More than one answer is possible.**

> I'm happy to hear that!    That's great to hear!
> That's a shame.    That's too bad.

1.  **Friend:** I got a new job! I'm really happy!

    **You:** _____

2.  **Friend:** I didn't pass my English test.

    **You:** _____

3.  **Friend:** My mother is not feeling very well.

    **You:** _____

4.  **Friend:** I learned to play the guitar, and I have a concert next week!

    **You:** _____

## C   *I think I'll get a job.*

**1** Complete the sentences with the words in the box and the simple past. Then number the pictures in the correct order.

| | | |
|---|---|---|
| buy a house | go to college | retire |
| ✓ get married | graduate from high school | start a career |
| get promoted | rent an apartment | start school |

# Dorothy was born in 1945. This is the story of her life . . .

She _got married_ to Leonard in 1970.

In 1967, she _____ .

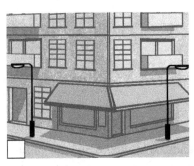

Dorothy _____ in 1950.

They _____ for five years.

She _____ 13 years later.

Dorothy _____ in 1980, and again in 1994.

She _____ in 2010.

Then, in 1975, they _____ .

She _____ in 1963.

## Now, she wants to travel around the world with her husband . . .

## 2 Match the sentences.

1. I'll never retire. ___e___
2. I may retire when I'm 65. _____
3. I might save enough money for a new car. _____
4. I'll save enough money for college by July. _____
5. I won't go to Mexico in the summer. _____
6. I might go to Spain next year. _____

a. That's the age my parents retired.
b. I start classes in September.
c. But I have to finish school first.
d. I need one to drive to work.
e. I love working!
f. It's too hot!

## 3 Complete the email. Use *will, won't,* or *might* and the words in parentheses. (++ = very certain, + = less certain)

Hello, Aunt Sarah!

How are you? I'm great. I have big plans for the future. I _'ll graduate_
(++ graduate) from high school next month. My brother _____ (+ come)
                                                              2
for my graduation. In June, my friend Christopher and I _____ (++ go) to
                                                                    3
Mexico. We _____ (++ stay) at our friend Mateo's house. Christopher
            4
_____ (+ leave) in July, but I _____ (++ stay) until
5                                          6
August. In September, I _____ (+ go) to college, or I
                        7
_____ (+ work) for a year first. I _____ (++ not decide)
8                                              9
until August.

Take care,
Ryan

## 4 Complete the email with the correct form of the words in parentheses. Use *will, won't,* or *may.*

Dear Ryan,

It was great to hear from you! You're graduating! Congratulations! I _may come_
                                                                        1
(come) to your party. I'm not sure. Paul _____ (have) a soccer game that
                                        2
weekend. We'll know for sure next week. But Uncle Dan and I want to take you to a new
Korean restaurant. We _____ (go) in May to celebrate! We don't have
                      3
many plans in May, so we have time. I know you _____ (love) Mexico!
                                                4
Uncle Dan and I _____ (not go) there this year because we need to save
                5
money. We don't know yet, but we _____ (go) to Canada. It will be
                                  6
cheaper because we can stay with friends in Canada.

See you soon!

Love,
Aunt Sarah

**5** Look at Hiro's notes. Then answer the questions about his plans.
Use *will* or *won't*.

---

### SUMMER PLANS

go to Vancouver to see friends, June   ✓ *buy ticket next week*
visit Uncle Kazu in Vancouver   ✗ *no time*
run a marathon, July   ✓ *running every day*
get a job   ✓ *look for a job, July*
take guitar lessons, August   ✗ *too expensive*

---

**Aya:** So, Hiro . . . Do you think you'll go to Vancouver this summer?

**Hiro:** <u>  *Yes, I will.*  </u> I'll buy my ticket next week.
               1

**Aya:** Great. And do you think you'll visit Uncle Kazu?

**Hiro:** _____ I'm not going to have time.
               2

**Aya:** Oh, do you think you'll run the marathon in July? I'll be in it!

**Hiro:** _____ I'm running every day now.
               3

**Aya:** We should practice together.

**Hiro:** That'd be great. We can run together in the morning or afternoon.

     I'm not working right now.

**Aya:** Really? Do you think you'll get a new job soon?

**Hiro:** _____ I'll look for a job in July when I get back
               4
     from Vancouver.

**Aya:** Hey, how about the guitar . . . Do you think you'll take those lessons?

**Hiro:** _____ They're too expensive. I need a job first!
               5

**6** Complete the sentences so they are true for you. Use *will, won't, may,* or *might*.

1. I _____ buy a new car next year.

2. I _____ get a new computer this year.

3. It _____ snow this week.

4. I _____ visit relatives next month.

5. My teacher _____ give us homework next week.

6.   **A:** Do you think you'll run a marathon next year?

    **You:** _____ .

7.   **A:** Do you think you'll ever be on a reality show?

    **You:** _____ .

# D Dreams and aspirations

**1** Read the webpage and article. Write the quotes in the correct place in the article.

Search by authors: A B C D E F G H I J K L M N O P Q R S T U V W X Y Z

**Search by subject:**
art
life
love
marriage
movies
politics
sports
work

**QUOTES OF THE DAY:**

*"Life isn't a matter of milestones, but of moments."*
– Rose Kennedy

*"All life is an experiment. The more experiments you make the better."*
– Ralph Waldo Emerson

*"There are people who have money and people who are rich."*
– Coco Chanel

## This week with Joan!

**Hello, readers!** This week I'm writing about life. I found three interesting quotes about life. One quote is " _____ ." I agree!
                                        1
I think it means you should experiment – change your habits and try new things – to make life interesting. So last week, I tried these experiments: I ate seaweed tacos, I ran a marathon, and I went salsa dancing! Next week, I might go skiing or buy a new computer.

Another person said, " _____ ." I really like this one.
                                    2
I don't have a million dollars, but I still feel rich. I have a great family and good friends. I enjoy a rich, happy life with them.

My favorite quote is " _____ ." This means the small
                                3
things in life are important. Sure, milestones are important, like graduating from college, starting a career, or getting married. But little things, moments, make life great. For example, I went shopping with my daughter. It wasn't a milestone, but we had fun, and I'll remember this day forever.

**So, my advice?** Work on your dreams and aspirations, but have fun, too. Life is short.

**2** Read the article again. Write P (past) or F (future) for Joan's experiences and plans.

1. eat seaweed tacos ___P___

2. run a marathon _____

3. go skiing _____

4. buy a new computer _____

# Credits